Gorilla Theory (The Art of Avoiding Project Delivery Disaster)

HENRY CHUKS

Spotlight Literary

Copyright © 2012 Henry Chuks

All rights reserved.

ISBN: 978-1484122358

DEDICATION

To everybody who has a project to deliver.

CONTENTS

	Acknowledgments	i
	Foreword by Gary Swart	Page 1
1	We Are all Project Managers	Page 11
2	The Baby Gorilla Scenario	Page 17
3	The Troop of Gorillas	Page 24
4	The Silverback Scenario	Page 37
5	Gorilla Theory Checklists	Page 53
6	People Skills	Page 56
7	Entrepreneurs & Start-Ups	Page 76
8	Making The Right Calls	Page 88
9	Summary & Close	Page 93
	Useful Reading	

Join the Gorilla Theory Community, Download the Checklists and Read More Case Studies.

The Gorilla Theory Meeting Organiser App for your iPhone, iPod Touch or iPad can Be Found in the Apple iTunes Store (search for **'Gorilla Theory'**). Available for Android smart phones from February 2013 (search for **'Gorilla Theory'** in Google's Play store).

www.gorillatheory.com

Gorilla Theory is a registered trademark.

Copyright © 2012 by Henry Chuks

All rights reserved under International and Pan-American Copyright Conventions.

Henry Chuks asserts the moral right to be identified as the author of this work. By payment of the required fees, you have been granted the non-exclusive, non-transferable right to access and read the text of this e-book on screen. No part of this text may be reproduced, transmitted, down-loaded, decompiled, reverse-engineered or stored in, or introduced into any information storage and retrieval system, in any form or by any means without the express written permission of the author or the publisher.

ACKNOWLEDGMENTS

Thanks to the very many entrepreneurs, start-up employees, and professionals who took the time to answer a few questions and to give me an insight into how they work and their views on better working practices when it comes to project management.

FOREWORD BY GARY SWART, CEO OF ODESK

As the world's largest online workplace, oDesk is home to hundreds of thousands of new projects each month — almost all of which occur between two people who have never met in person and never will. We focus on three pillars of online work relationships — hiring, managing and paying — but often a disproportionate amount of attention is paid to the first and last pillar, with "managing" almost an implicit assumption.

This is a major disjoint, as I venture to say that managing may be the most important. I have seen millions of projects succeed (and a good number fail) due to project management savviness or ineptitude.

Online work is an extreme example — time zone differences, language barriers and varying cultural approaches to projects are just a few of the factors that make effective project management so indispensable. But even within the walls of oDesk's office in Silicon Valley, skilled project management is crucial to our success. Our business lives or dies based on whether we have a diligent focus on strategic priorities, as well as proactive management of people, time and resources.

Still, for all its importance, the art of effective project management is typically seen as just that — an art. There are great 'artists' out there as well as those workers who aren't aware of the art they are being asked to perform. I have observed a common behaviour in project owners where they feel that creating effective relationships with their team members is not important or even unnecessary. The truth is that effective team member relationships are of huge significance to the success of a project.

With this book, Henry successfully identifies and gives guidance on improving the important areas that help projects get delivered more efficiently. It is easy to be overwhelmed by a project and to think you are just not good at delivering tasks.

Gorilla Theory addresses the dire need for structured, actionable, yet very practical guidance in project management — Henry does a great job of breaking down an ambiguous topic into manageable advice, providing tremendous insight as well as helpful examples that will make the great project professionals even better, and help the rest perform far better in any project they are involved with.

This indispensable guide to project management has arrived not a moment too soon.

INTRODUCTION

Let's begin with what this book is about. Gorilla Theory (The Art of Avoiding Project Delivery Disaster) tackles the questions:

1) How can I be better at delivering projects?

2) How can I prevent project delivery disasters?

Why do I think this important to you? Project management is a part of everyday life: your work life and your personal life.

Let's look at weddings for example. Have you ever been given the job of organising the wedding for a close friend or family member? What about a stag or hen party? Organising these events are huge tasks, involving arranging venues, parties, gifts, families, food, gifts, friends, cars, personalities and more. As well as a stiff drink, you will desperately need strong and effective project management skills to not only ensure that all of the intricate elements of the grand occasion all come together as they should, but to also ensure that you still have a friend after the ordeal.

The smiles and joy of the actual happy day often belie a

trouble-strewn build-up, filled with disputes and frustration. Organising weddings does not have to be a painful project.

Being organised enough to deliver tasks asked of you or to manage people who need to get separate things done for a single goal is massively relevant if you're running a business, but also if you're just trying to organise something in life that is very important.

How many nightmare projects have you been a part of? If you are an adult with workplace experience, you will undoubtedly be able to cast your mind back to projects that involved stress, tension, hard-to-meet deadlines, clashing personalities and more problems. If you are still studying, you may be thinking of an academic project that went awry, or exam preparation or course work that did not go according to plan. Perhaps you may have organised a large party, a business event. It is easy to remind ourselves of the problems we have experienced in past projects.

Projects that go bad can have serious financial implications. For example, just look at the UK's National Health Service (NHS) IT Infrastructure improvement project that was closed down in 2011 with a checklist full of unachieved objectives and £3billion frittered away.

A crucial part of the systems overhaul was the digitising of patient records – something that would have provided massive benefits to hospitals, doctors, and the sick and injured who need medical help. Billions of pounds spent and no improvements achieved!

There are more than financial implications to projects that are unsuccessful. True human disaster can result.

Malcolm Gladwell's *Outliers* offers a fascinating insight into the reasons behind the seeming prominence and success of selected individuals and certain groups of people. In the chapter concerning his *'Ethnic Theory of Plane Crashes'*, Gladwell surmises that plane crashes are *'much more likely to be the result of an accumulation of minor difficulties and seemingly trivial malfunctions'* than due to systems or mechanical failures.

The author broadens the target of this reasoning to most industrial accidents, recalling the infamous near nuclear meltdown in the U.S. of Pennsylvania's Three Mile Island nuclear station – the worst accident in U.S. commercial nuclear power plant history. The leakage of radioactive material and the ensuing near disaster were caused by a series of unrelated events that were missed and led to more serious issues. Difficulties arising from seemingly unrelated events such as these must somehow be pulled together, controlled and managed before they can lead to catastrophes. Making a point of being vigilant is one of Gorilla Theory's foundations.

The causes of the plane crashes and the Three Mile Island nuclear accident could have been avoided by means of rigorous checks, disciplined vigilance and greater team work, all led by a disciplined and vigilant Project Manager. This may sound far too simple a solution for such major problems, but the power of what is proposed in this book lies in the simplicity and transferability of the underlying principles. Complexity is on the way out in life and in business, and simple solutions win more engagement and commitment. Have you noticed how mobile apps and websites can be more intuitive and easier to use than the websites they are based on?

Mobile has to be simple and intuitive as the user by default is on the move and has less attention to spare. The mobile platform forces simplicity. Project Management should do the same.

I have polled hundreds of entrepreneurs, professionals and students, as well as management consultants, from firms such as Accenture, Deloitte, ghSMART & Company, KPMG, Logica, and PwC. I wanted to get a feel for how individuals, business founders and employees, plus the consultancy firms who support businesses, approach getting things done and managing projects. I was surprised at the number of common themes involving the human elements of delivering projects were mentioned in the many interviews and survey results.

Later on in the book I explain that the title 'project manager' is not just for professional specialist project managers or consultants, but can be applied to anybody who has a series of tasks to deliver.

One of the main objectives of this book is to provide timeless and relevant information on being a project delivery linchpin and how to prevent or lessen the pain of difficult projects.

As a project delivery linchpin you can improve the way you deliver any project you undertake ensuring that disasters are averted when delivering a project so that you – the Project Manager – can sail through to the end of the project without any surprises and with all of the benefits you intended at the start of the project.

This is not a technical book laden with methodology-speak and unnecessary jargon. If you work in the web, software or digital sectors then great, but you will derive just as much benefit – if not more – if you work in other business sectors, including entrepreneurs thinking about launching a business or web application of your own.

Global businesses of all sizes and age are in a new era of project delivery. The need to quickly bring a new product or service to market or to a 'ready-to-use' state has become heightened in line with the 'now', 'instant gratification' demands of the expectant consumer. The stakes are high for the established company as well as the boot-strapping start-up to get delivery right, and the cost of failure is increasing all the time.

For any business that doesn't have a specialist project management guru or crack-team there needs to be accessible and easy to implement ways to help the untrained and inexperienced employees to succeed in delivering projects. Solving this problem was the genesis of Gorilla Theory.

Based on personal experience as a seasoned project manager having delivered millions of pounds worth technology products and services over the last twelve years, I have found that there are no magic bullets or secret strategies to being good at getting things done or delivered. Just as Eric Reis's Lean Start-Up movement focuses on efficiencies and practicalities of getting a new product or service off the ground, Gorilla Theory zeroes in on the behaviours' you need to adopt to be a project management star.

Gorilla Theory is a new way of visualising what you need to do day to day in the successful completion of your projects. You will benefit from having a clear picture of the tasks you need to get done, and the project as a whole. If you have a task to do (be it designing and programming the new Facebook, or planning a wedding) Gorilla Theory applies a set of common sense principles that aims to help anybody to better understand their role as project manager or project team member, and to be more adept at getting their tasks done for the benefit of their project as a whole.

People skills (particularly the focus on YOU) are the central focus of the model. Gorilla Theory also emphasises the use of checklists to help the project manager to be more alert to the issues that may arise in any project.

The full list of Gorilla Theory core principles are:

- Discipline
- Awareness
- Communication
- Vigilance
- People Skills

Gorilla Theory categorises and visualises projects as:

- **Baby Gorillas** (Small Projects)
- **A Troop of Gorillas** (Multiple Projects)
- **A Silverback** (Large Projects / Programme of Work)

In the coming chapters, I will explain how to visualise the projects that you are working on or are about to embark on.

I have made the assumption that all projects you are involved with are a team effort. Of course, this is not always the case as you may work on some projects by yourself, so when I mention consulting with senior management or client account managers or senior stakeholders as part of the disaster-avoidance solutions, take it that **YOU** are the head of the project and that **YOU** need to take a time out to brainstorm, review or assess and then formulate an action plan.

This guide is purposefully not text-heavy as it is designed to be a quick reference that you can constantly dip into when needed.

I'm a big fan of insightful business books and guides, but in the heat of the battle – delivering a project or a new business – when help is needed, it needs to be quickly available, and clear case studies and action bullet points are a very effective way to give urgently needed information.

    Here's to your successful projects.

"Stand calm, firm, and united in this time of trial. The task will be hard. There may be dark days ahead, and war can no longer be confined to the battlefield. But we can only do the right as we see the right, and reverently commit our cause to God. If one and all we keep resolutely faithful to it, ready for whatever service or sacrifice it may demand, then, with God's help, we shall prevail."

King George VI's broadcast from Buckingham Palace, on the outbreak of war with Germany September 3, 1939, 6pm

1. WE ARE ALL PROJECT MANAGERS

You should never rest on your laurels or be complacent when trying to get something done that involves the organising and managing of people, delivery schedules and budgets. A project is a collection of tasks required to achieve something or build something (be it a product or service), and is a powerful entity. You can you rest when delivery is complete, not during. To do so invites delivery disaster. As I mentioned earlier, managing projects permeates our work and personal lives. The less stress we have managing our work in the office and on our own time, the more energy can be spent in peace or having more fun.

TV shows such as Dragon's Den and The Apprentice highlight how the team leaders shoulder the primary burden of delivering a project successfully and can get castigated for their supposed failings as a person manager, for their decision making and planning of the tasks set out.

The Apprentice is a show created for viewer entertainment, but the core reasons for the failure of a project and the people in the project team are laid bare for analysis. How many times have you watched the show and thought that the candidate chosen as project manager seems like a reasonably competent and nice enough person before their composure and grip on their project team members and the task itself slips beyond repair? These beleaguered team leaders composure quickly unravels before they are invariably savaged by their own team members in the boardroom at the end of every show; animosity and finger pointing is given full voice in the boardroom while Sir Alan Sugar observes with his own management advisers.

It is easy to denigrate the efforts of the appointed team leaders and the team members themselves from an armchair. I can relate to having bore the brunt of several of the personality types on projects I have been a part of, and some of the chaotic meetings that happen on the show. Yes, it is a cleverly edited show for entertainment, but the same elements of lack of communication and teamwork, lack of praising and building trust and morale, as well as selfishness simply mirrors offices and businesses around the globe.

When people in a team do not get along, the team suffers and the project suffers. The Apprentice magnifies typical human behaviour in the delivery of a project. If you observe the contestants of the show and wonder if you perform in a similar way in the workplace then rest assured, there are steps you can take to improve your performance in delivering tasks and projects in the workplace or with people outside of the office.

In these harsher economic times it is common for employers to load their staff with increasingly bigger workloads. Managing time and projects in parallel is an increasing need for many. Start-ups are not immune. It is the bootstrapping culture for all involved in the nascent company to multi-task and fight to produce as much value for every last coin of the start-up budget or investment. Effective delivery management should be as essential and robust as the business plan or the product idea.

Do not be put off by the use of the term project manager or its equivalents in this guide. In the Gorilla Theory world a project manager is a loose term expanded to include any person involved in the delivery of a task project. Thus, in addition to a specialist project manager, a designer, programmer, account manager, student, accountant, general office worker, business owner and multiple other roles can be viewed as a project manager in terms of what they need to produce, oversee, or what they have a stake in seeing delivered.

Sure, actual project management professionals are likely to benefit most from this guide, but, I encourage you to see yourself as the project manager of your own work and your own responsibilities in your role if this is not your job title. This book is designed to give you a different perspective on how to visualise your workload and to-do list, and to provide helpful guidance on how to get projects delivered safely, as well as advising you on what can go wrong in the delivery process. Gorilla Theory will help you in being more aware and proactive in ensuring that your projects or tasks stay on track.

I will not delve deeply into the known, standardised project management and delivery methodologies such as Prince2, Agile, ITIL, Waterfall and the rest. They are all very important, but Gorilla Theory is about the forgotten layers in project delivery – the person managing the project, the people involved in getting the project done, and monitoring and vigilance. In addition, most people who are involved in projects or getting their own tasks done have not been trained in project management principles and are likely to never receive such training. Gorilla Theory is an approach that you can adopt and refine for your own use after reading this book.

I love reading a good business book, learning from case studies of other peoples' experiences, and doing courses to further my knowledge of project management methods, but in the regular working day and for client consultancy projects, I prefer to use reference guides that are very accessible, that are incisive and get to the point quickly to help when I'm in a fix. This is why this book is modeled more as a reference manual. This is not a book that you need to read cover to cover. You can, but you can also dive in to the necessary sections according to the issues you are having or the guidance you need at the particular time.

Gorilla Theory is the output of my learning, successes, failures and observations. I only hope that it provides the tools you need to avoid the Scylla and Charybdis of disaster and delivery pain in your projects.

THE ART OF AVOIDING PROJECT DELIVERY DISASTER

(Disaster Prevention Tactics for Project Management)

Gorilla Theory is founded on FIVE key principles that sit above any project delivery methodology or bespoke process. People skills and emotional intelligence underpins Gorilla Theory and enhances the PEOPLE layer of a project ecosystem.

- Discipline
- Awareness
- Comms
- Vigilance

↕ ↕ ↕ ↕

People Skills & Emotional Intelligence

↕ ↕ ↕ ↕

The Project Manager & The Project People

↕ ↕ ↕ ↕

Project Delivery Processes / Methodology

Gorilla Theory will certainly help you understand the pressures and working environment of an actual project manager or the person who leads projects in your team or workplace, and create (I hope) an empathy for your fellow project team members. It will pay dividends in working relationships and better performing project delivery processes if you become more familiar with how to a project manager works and how to avoid disasters. Better the devil you know and all that...or is it keep your enemies close...?

Without any particular planning and care, some projects will get delivered on time and to specification without major issues, without conflict by luck or for reasons outside of your influence. This is pure luck. In most cases, when you are poorly prepared, a project will fail to deliver on time and to a suitable standard of the required specification and there will be significant issues.

Following an effective process and - where possible - learning from previous delivery mistakes makes a huge difference to the success of a project delivery. It also pays to be self-aware, being able to put ego and subjective feelings aside to make the right decisions.

Gorilla Theory will also help you to understand the power and importance of team work and intra-team relationships. Projects are delivered by a mixture of bespoke workflow procedures and established delivery methods such as SCRUM and the like. There is a necessary focus on these processes, but the human element is the one you are unlikely to read about in methodology books or be taught about extensively on methodology courses.

Learning to balance the process side and the human side usually takes time and experience. Being an effective project manager is like becoming a good driver. You have to know some of the theory, and you learn how to drive more smoothly and better after many hours on the road. Gorilla Theory should help you to put in place the personal plan that keeps you one step ahead with every project you are involved with.

"A goal without a plan is just a wish."

Antoine de Saint-Exupery

2 THE BABY GORILLA SCENARIO

Baby gorillas may seem cute and cuddly and easy to handle, but they are far more complex and stronger than their appearance suggests. A baby gorilla can overwhelm you with demands for feeding, attention, protection, cleaning and what's more, a baby is constantly growing! Taking care of one baby prepares you for a new one, but as a baby grows, its demands change. You need to keep your wits about you at all times.

What is it?

Baby gorillas are small projects that are initially deemed straightforward, even easy, to deliver. What happens is that a lack of vigilance and respect for proper processes cause a lack of attention to detail and scoping and the baby gorilla grows into a powerful adult project that overpowers the project manager.

Alternatively, some projects are simply classed as basic or easy-to-do and the project goes in to action with this misconception. Then it becomes apparent that there are major complexities or obstacles and/or lack of information of the scope that could seriously delay the delivery of the project or even make it impractical or unwise to even attempt.

A baby gorilla can morph quickly into a troop of gorillas (more on troops later). For a budding entrepreneur, the big idea for a new product or service can be classed as a baby gorilla; the planning and implementing of the big idea is a troop of gorillas (more about them later), and the new product or service once it is launched is a silverback gorilla (again, more about that later).

How to spot one

Be wary of ANY project deemed easy-to-do, basic, small, or business as usual, and be cautious and investigative when it is assumed that enough is known of what needs to be done (the full requirements and delivery specifications). If you are given a project such as this check if all the requirements are gathered (and approved) and that the scope has been signed-off by the necessary people.

Baby gorillas usually occur when the precise details and approvals are not gathered, defined and approved, and (usually) not enough time is given for the delivery. In the new media agency landscape, baby gorillas tend to be media campaign assets (such as advertising banners), HTML newsletters, microsite, site/page update-style projects (such as changing the logo or colour of a hyperlink onmouseover background).

What to do? The Baby Gorilla Action Plan

Wisdom is a blessing and experience is invaluable. What I should have done in my early days as a project manager being handed baby gorilla projects (and what I would advise any person to do) is:

1) To gather ALL the information you have on the task(s) that need to be done, and assign contact names to every piece of information you have received on the project (you should always go back to the source of information for any clarification).

2) As soon as possible, have a meeting with the senior management and the lead client account manager for the project to get an absolute understanding of what is believed to be the deliverable(s) and what are the knowledge gaps.

3) Once the knowledge gaps are identified, nothing else should happen until the project is correctly scoped and approved internally and by the client (YES, this will take time, but you simply have to know exactly what needs to be delivered).

4) Advise a realistic delivery schedule based on the full scope as you now understand it and get internal and client buy-in for the realistic delivery date (if the due date is written in stone you need senior approval for extra resources to get the job done within the time allowed)

5) Manage the delivery well – watch over each and every milestone and ensure all tasks are being done on time.

Baby Gorilla Solution Risks

I'm sure a great many of you who have delivered media campaigns will scoff at point three above. I've been there. It is easier to say what should happen than to do what is needed.

From the benefit of my experiences, excellent, good, bad, and the horrible, what I will advise is that you must have conviction in pushing for the above steps to happen where possible. It is far easier to be swept along with the tide than to grab at the opportunity to make a stand and admit that you do not have enough information and that you need to fully understand what is going on. This can usually be attributed to:

(i) a subtly bullying culture (such as in busy digital development agencies, and investment banks) where you are expected to just 'get on with it' and get things done

(ii) a lack of effective delivery processes to support delivering projects well in the first place, and,

(iii) the imperative to take care of the client and skip to their beat in order to claim their money to the detriment of effective delivery processes and to the chagrin and detriment of the project manager. The client + money first culture.

Sure, the project manager will likely shoulder the brunt of the blame for late-delivery or non-delivery, but if you make every effort to call a halt to impending disaster and advise on solutions to remedy the problem, then at least you have a fighting chance of bringing about positive change that will help right the project. It does not always work.

In the example of the huge social media platform, nothing I said to the project board seemed to make any difference. My words of warning were gratefully noted, but the most senior managers were locked in a pattern of non-action behaviour that was leading to ruin. **ALWAYS** call an immediate halt at even the merest hint of delivery disaster.

In digital development agencies in particular, there is a culture of 'just get it done for the client' amongst senior management.

Baby Gorilla Case Study

In 2010 I was working for a well-to-do digital development agency that specialises in digital marketing and social media for the family and entertainment sectors. Within a week of joining, I was assigned the delivery of (what seemed to be) a straightforward digital media campaign assets (website advertising banners such as: banners, skyscrapers, MPUs and YouTube skins) for a set of European countries. I was told that it was a simple baby-sitting task as most of the scoping and solution-definition work had been done.

I played rugby to a decent level as a very young man. My first coaches always told us to pass the ball on as smooth and flat a path as possible to give your teammate the best chance of advancing play or to score. They counseled against slowly thrown and looping passes – commonly known as hospital passes. These types of passes are so named because the intended recipient of the pass is obliged to catch the ball, but because of the slow trajectory of the pass, the defending side's players will find it easier to tackle the attacker when he catches the ball and will usually do so with extreme force.

I felt like I had been lobbed a hospital pass with this project. I was intent on impressing my new employers, showing how I can add value, but I struggled immediately.

The marketing campaign was for the promotion of a highly anticipated fantasy adventure film starring Jake Gyllenhaal (Disney's The Prince of Persia). The handover meeting I had with the incumbent project manager – who was leaving for a holiday the next day – lasted no more than 10 minutes. New to the company and with no further background information on the media campaign, I did not ask the departing project manager the necessary questions to get a full picture and to discover the knowledge gaps in the delivery...there was several unknowns!

The departing project manager had not only failed to correctly list all the ad formats that were required and the specification of all the ad formats, but he also did not inform me of all the current design work locations and work done locations, never mind the advert trafficking specifications needed.

We had two weeks to deliver all the correct ads for six EU

countries. What we also did not know was that all these ads had to have the correct DoubleClick ad-tagging implemented. Thus, the specifications for all the ads had to be gathered and approved, the design and build work had to be planned and then streamed into the agency's work stream, and then the work had to be done, and then tested, and then approved internally and by the end client (the world's biggest children's fantasy business) and then the approved assets had to be delivered to the countries and deployed to the ad-trafficking systems.

It was a huge amount of items to get through in two weeks. When you add to the mix the usual resource constraints of a busy agency that cannot just drop everything to deliver one project, the disapproval of a very high-profile end client, and the general lack of knowledge as to what was asked for and by when and it adds up to the usual late delivery disaster that is so common within digital agencies and software/application providers. The client and advertising partners applied pressure as they wanted to assess the designs and then approve them when they were happy, and then get the assets in good time for the launch of the film and the planned advert go-live dates scheduled with various advert publishing agencies and media partners.

What happened? We delivered late of course – to all the countries. I was fighting fire from the outset and never got a true handle on the whole project (I had also been given three other major projects to manage alongside this hornet's nest).

Popular Baby Gorilla Examples – Social Networking Technology

Baby Gorilla Handled Well: LinkedIn's iPad app. The team at

LinkedIn took their time and did not rush in, getting the user experience as optimal as possible before launching. The iPad app was very well received and is gaining a lot of user traction.

Baby Gorilla Handled Badly: Facebook's early mobile app (much pilloried for usability issues, having bugs, and for being slow). The world's most popular social network put on mobile should have been a huge instant hit right? In terms of download numbers it was, but Facebook did not align the user experience and performance of the mobile version of the website with a mind to real mobile needs and usability. More time should have been taken in researching how Facebook SHOULD translate and perform on smaller screens, as well as allowing for commercial (advertising) gains to be made in the mobile sector.

"The simplest rule of crisis management is to have a simple, clear, unified strategy."

US Treasury Secretary, Tim Geithner

3 THE TROOP OF GORILLAS SCENARIO

Have you seen Planet of the Apes or Congo? Gangs of angry apes and gorillas are a scary proposition.

What is it?

A troop of gorillas is a situation in which you – the project manager – have more than one project happening at the same time. At times like these there is the danger that the projects can start going wrong because your attention for each project is split and – therefore – reduced.

When one baby gorilla becomes too boisterous, you can quickly lose control of the whole pack and be overrun. When one project becomes difficult to deal with, it can take your focus away from others as well as take up much more of your time, leaving less focus and time for the others. A troop of gorillas causes a very quick escalation of problems and creates a vicious cycle that will not get better by itself.

The modern office environment and that of start-ups, small and young businesses foster a culture of frenzied activity and multi-tasking, particularly in times of recession such as we are experiencing right now. Managers and employees can all be overloaded with multiple to-dos. The focus is on getting as much done as possible, and there is usually not an equal emphasis on delivering to a robust standard and delivering well. Task overloading can lead to underperformance from even the most experienced or senior workers and this decrease in performance quality has been recognised as a new neurological phenomenon called **Attention Deficit Trait** (ADT).

Attention Deficit Trait is increasingly common, and a by-product of the modern work place. It is characterised by *distractibility, inner frenzy, and impatience.

ADT prevents managers and workers from clarifying priorities, making smart decisions, and managing their time. This condition turns otherwise talented and competent performers into harassed underachievers. Handling a number of projects at the same time can often reduce your focus on due process and quality. The more projects you are involved with, the more meetings, the more issues, bugs, planning, reporting, milestone watching, resource management, stakeholder management, scope defining, scope watching etc. Everything multiplies and stress can rise quickly.

How to spot a Troop of Gorillas

You know if you have a troop of gorillas when you have more than one project and you are worried that – with at least one of them – there is unknown scope and/or there is resource availability or reliability issue and a deadline that looks unrealistic at best, impossible at worst. This is compounded by lack of help from colleagues who could advise on some background to the projects or the delivery process as used by the employer - tricks of the trade even. Scope issues are an immediate red flag, and are a cause for concern.

RULE: Always know precisely what is required and precisely what is unknown when it comes to a project scope. It's the unknown that usually trips you up and causes the biggest problems.

*'Overloaded Circuits, Why Smart People Underperform', by Edward M. Hallowell, HBR.org

RULE: Always have the entire scope defined and approved. Not doing so leads to infamous scope creep or the nasty surprise of more work being required than has been scoped, planned and - in some cases - costed for. If you do not have a thorough and approved scope, prepare to fail or do not be surprised if you have difficulty in delivering.

Being concerned with resource availability and/or reliability can mean that you have either NOT added contingency for the lack of man power or the lack of effort of the resource, or you are unable to plan with contingency in mind due to client agreements or service level agreements.

When you are suffering a troop of gorillas, you will feel a constant level of stress, panic and paranoia. Consistently dealing with a troop of gorillas can quickly lead to burnout if this is your usual pace.

What to do? The Troop of Gorillas action plan

A troop of gorillas' situation is one that calls for precise planning. Specifically, you as the project manager for all the projects need to manage your time effectively and to give each project designated attention throughout a working day and working week.

Day planners may seem very old-school and tedious to do but they work. Without bias having an effective daily schedule will keep you focused and productive. You will be less likely to miss any issues on a project if you plan to look at it at designated times on a regular basis.

I am speaking in very general terms, but the daily planner can be very detailed indeed. You can use the project delivery plans for each project to feed into the daily planner so each milestone, review or approval gateway is not missed. Daily planners take time to do, but they are well worth the effort.

If you are amidst a pack of gorillas that is starting to overthrow you, then – borrowing from the Baby Gorilla scenario – the most important thing you can do is to immediately CALL A HALT. Stopping may seem like the most difficult, counter-productive thing to do in a project, but it is one of the - if not far and away the most - rationale, healing things you can do.

Just STOP and assess.

Raise the alarm with the key internal stakeholders (the client does not need to be contacted as it is an internal issue) and advise that you need some time or assistance to get back on track so that you avoid a huge mess. Yes, I DID say ask for help. It took me several years to realise that there is no loss of face or credibility in admitting that you are or are about to be overrun.

It was a pride thing with me, but I learned that waving the white flag actually shows foresight and professional concern for the delivery of the project(s).

If you think I'm wrong, think back to projects that you led that went badly and in which delivery dates were missed. If you had flagged early on that there was a problem with the delivery management, or that you were struggling to cope, and help arrived or you were given time to right yourself, wouldn't this have helped you?

It is usually far better to flag issues very early than get blamed at the end and try to belatedly raise concerns you had during the project. This latter scenario shows a lack of leadership of a project and lack of skill in management of projects.

A second element to help such a situation is having great working relationships with the various project team members.

Being on friendly terms and having a foundation of some trust with your planners, designers, developers and testers as well as management can really ease the pain of a stuttering project. The team members are more likely to lend a helping hand and find that extra time to get things done or get things ready. A good relationship with management means that if you communicate with them regularly and work to a high standard, if you come to them needing help or support, they will be more open to helping.

On any given project, **ALWAYS** make sure all team members know who you are and what your role is in the project. Tell them all how you like to work and what you appreciate and dislike. It makes you more human and accessible. You may scoff, but increasingly, good interpersonal skills massively aid the smooth running of a project. In many a digital agency or software firm, designers, developers and architects can relay stories of the one-track-minded, blunt and unfriendly project manager who they hated working with on any project.

The relentless, shoulder-hovering presence, and the blank-eyed repetition of requirements and progress questions. Friction between project team members leads to the overall strain on the project as a whole. The more strain, the more likely things are to go wrong. Being nice (but still firm and decisive) is a valuable lubricant that keeps the delivery machine moving along.

Gorilla Troop Action Points

1) Gather ALL the information you have on the task(s) at hand and assign contact names to who has given whatever information on the project

1b) Meet and greet ALL key internal stakeholders for each project and inform them who you are and at what stage you are joining the project and how you like to work. Ask them where they think the project is – in terms of status – and what they are expecting

2) Immediately have a meeting with the senior management and the lead client account manager for the project and to get an absolute understanding of what is believed to be the deliverable(s) and what are the knowledge gaps

3) Create a Daily Planner and include touch points for each project that references the delivery schedule for that project and its individual issues and risks and status

4) Advise a realistic delivery schedule based on the full scope and get internal and client buy-in (if the due date is written in stone you need senior approval for extra resources to get the job done within the time allowed)

5) Manage the delivery well - watch over each and every milestone and ensure all phases are being done on time.

How to Reduce Gorilla Troop Project Overload Stress:

1) Take some 'me' time and think about positive things or things you are passionate about

2) Ease stress with regular outlets

3) Take care of your brain - it does a lot of processing work every day. Give it some rest with a good amount of sleep for you or just put it on auto pilot.

4) Plan for ADT. Set aside strict time to plan and organise and at least keep abreast of issues

What to do When You Feel Overwhelmed

>> Stop what you are doing. Slow down. Take the time you need to comprehend what is going on, to listen, to ask questions, and to digest what's been said so that you don't get confused and send your brain into panic.

>> Do an easy rote task: Reset your watch, write a note about a neutral topic (such as a description of your house), read a few dictionary definitions, do a short crossword puzzle.

>> Move around: Go up and down a flight of stairs or walk briskly.

>> Ask for help, delegate a task, or brainstorm with a colleague. In short, do not worry alone.

Troop of Gorillas Solution Risks

Adopting the 'I need help' strategy for the first time can lead to disappointment from senior management and peers who simply expect you to handle everything thrown at you with skill and enthusiasm. Resource unhappiness can stem from them being under-the-gun themselves with an overflowing workload. If you need help, they may have to provide the assistance and they may not want to.

Management can take a dim view of a project manager admitting that there is a problem because they expect that they hire people who can do the job effortlessly and do not like to deal with problems. They want things to get done and then to make money from the clients. Whilst I believe that the solution is based upon more than enough experience, both personal and observed, some management folk offer no support or sympathy upon a cry for help.

The outcome could be that putting your hand up and declaring that you are in trouble could cause a terminal lack of confidence amongst the management. Unfair? Of course, but not all managers are good managers with a healthy, broad view. This truth may be tough to take, but it is never preferable for a project or your reputation to go down in flames simply because you didn't want to admit that things were out of your control. As my dear father always used to say, 'pride comes before the fall'.

Troop of Gorillas Case Study

The best example I can give still brings me out in a cold sweat. It's from my time – in 2010 – at the same digital development agency of the Baby Gorilla case study.

Their client roster included Proctor and Gamble, NBC Universal and Disney. After three rounds of interviews and being told that everybody who was on the various panels really took to me and wanted me to join, join I did. Within my first two weeks, I had been given four major, multi-faceted projects – all with the flimsiest of handovers.

The first was the build of a new online Movie-on-Demand website and it's supporting CMS and film inventory management tool (three weeks away from launch), the build of a new interactive online game for a new children's toy product (LEGO; the project was in the initial planning and scoping phase), the design and build of a Nordics marketing microsite for 4 countries for a popular snacks brand (also in scoping phase), and - the really scary one - the delivery of marketing assets for the launch of the Prince of Persia film - due in three weeks from when I was handed the project (the aforementioned baby Gorilla case study).

Senior project manager or not, that is a lot of work for the most organised delivery professional. What made this near impossible was primarily the TV-on-Demand website as I had no handover notes no scope document, the backend and CMS was built by a freelancer who had not engaged with the project manager who I took over from and was resistant to regular communications and reports on the bug-fixing.

The previous project manager became very ill before I joined and to add to that, she was leaving within a few weeks of me joining. She became too ill to come in to the office and give me a proper handover, so I had to run with the project and try and get it done. There was no style-guide to refer to or much background information.

I was told to speak with the in-house freelancer team (the developer and the designer), the inventory data controllers (a third-party software firm), liaise with the client on progress and to organise user acceptance testing, and to manage the bugs and issues lists and get the site live. In comparison to the film launch media campaign baby gorilla case study given in the previous chapter, the movie-on-demand website project was very manageable.

I have relied on good people skills when managing projects for several years, and I found that making the effort to get to know the freelancers and to explain to them how I work and what needed to get done helped to build trust and to increase their productivity.

The media campaign project turned out to be a troop of gorillas on its own. In short, six formats of a digital advert were required for six countries. What my insubstantial handover did not detail included:

- The design specification for all the advert formats

- All the source files for the designs

- The specification for the animation files

- The advert-trafficking codes required for integration into the banners

- A list of all the various country contacts

- The required dates for delivery for each country

- The ad campaign technical contacts and integration specs (particular to the UK launch campaign)

All of these details I had to find out on the fly. There was major stress. At the same time as learning about my new colleagues and the internal processes, I was on the spot for a high profile delivery of which I had nowhere near enough information. I had to pretty much harass my colleagues for help - they were very busy with their own projects. I had to stress out the designers and developers with continuous requests for information, requests for amends, and delivery, without having the approved design spec to hand.

A lot of my comrades proved very helpful and I was extremely grateful for that.

Did I get everything on track ad delivered on time? No. Not even close. I can still vividly recall how wretched I began to feel after a few weeks in this new job – getting in early in the mornings, leaving late in the evening. When you have that much pressure to deliver and the sheer volume of tasks and people and reporting to keep on top of, it is a huge challenge that would test the thickest skinned individual.

The initial countries that launched the film (UK included) suffered a delay in having the full digital marketing campaigns. It was unavoidable in the circumstances. I felt like a lamb to the slaughter. This agency did not subscribe to a particular delivery methodology. They had developed and stuck to their own bespoke processes but I found no comfort or support in their methods with such a baptism of fire.

The movie-on-demand website launched on time though, as did the multi-level, online LEGO game project. These were positive outcomes, but my reputation and health took big hits.

I felt burned out after a month. It was not a fun time and this most difficult of beginnings in a new job left a very negative impression of me and of my skills amongst my colleagues. I did not recover from this (and more importantly, I did not want to – I wanted to get the hell out and walked serenely away when given the gentle push).

At no time did my project load dip under maximum capacity busy and running on empty. This is the way for many digital/software consultancies. The workloads do not necessarily have to change (though it would be nice in some cases), but the process for managing projects has to change.

By the time I left the agency, they were restructuring how they operate and the processes for each unit (development, design, and project management). I hope for their sake that the restructure brings about greater clarity on the delivery and collaboration process so that they can become more efficient. Sure, they did not lose the clients I worked on and continue to win new business, but they would gain more productivity from their delivery workers if they worked in a better way.

The better the processes, the better the project delivery. The better the project delivery, the more time is available for more projects. To point out the obvious, more projects = more money. In the time I was with this digital development agency, they lost well over 100,000GBP in errors caused by defective delivered projects. I was responsible for some of those losses and that is not a nice feeling to be accountable for significant commercial disasters.

Hopefully the restructure has produced the necessary reflection that enough is enough. If the senior management came to the mindset that they were fed up of losing money because of mistakes and delivering late sometimes and our staff are getting burnt out consistently. Time for change.

Popular Troop of Gorillas Examples - Sport

A Troop of Gorillas Scenario Handled Well: The Miami Heat basketball team of 2011-12. The current NBA champions returned from finals defeat in 2011, stronger and with more effective play from their three main stars and bench players to capture the title, whilst managing their much vaunted three superstars – LeBron James, Dwayne Wade, and Chris Bosh – and heightened expectations). The Heat retained their title in

June 2013.

A Troop of Gorillas Scenario Handled Badly: The Manchester City football (soccer) team of 2010-2011. Despite over one hundred million pounds invested in new players, the new manager (Roberto Mancini) failed to make the team gel effectively enough to win the English Premiership (in contrast with the instant success of Jose Mourinho with Chelsea in 2004-2005, when he joined as the new head coach and steered them to the title at the first time of asking after a summer 2004 investment of sixty million pounds).

"You are beaten. It is useless to resist. Don't let yourself be destroyed...."

DARTH VADER, THE EMPIRE STRIKES BACK

4 THE SILVERBACK PROJECT SCENARIO

The big daddy of project problems. The fully grown, hugely powerful and intimidating Silverback gorilla needs to be handled with care. They are awesome just to look at. Only very silly people think they could walk up to a Silverback without any background information or prolonged analysis and stay unmolested in close proximity.

Large projects need a lot of attention and need to be broken down into manageable chunks. In short, do not try to be a hero and handle a large project on your own. As Messrs. Knight, Thomas and Angus advise in the excellent *Project Management for Profit*, 'there are too many undifferentiated tasks' in large projects. These 'undifferentiated tasks' are given the tag 'blobs' in their book. They go on to say that a blob is 'a large task or series of tasks required for the project, but with details that are poorly defined and hence poorly understood.'

What is it?

A Silverback project is characterised by a combination of or ALL of: being complex in terms of scope, having a very high-profile and a high budget, and having several small projects and project groups dependent on one another. Easy examples are planning a wedding, launching a new hardware product, setting up a new business, building a house.

How to spot a Silverback

ALL large, complicated projects are Silverbacks by default! Staring a new business, organising a wedding, moving home, leading or being involved in a large budget programme are all constitute examples of Silverbacks. Start with this mindset and you will be primed to plan more effectively at the beginning or pick up the pieces and troubleshoot as soon as you join the project.

I have had various project roles in multi-million pound, hundreds of millions of euro budget projects. In all cases I joined some time after the project had been started. I could quickly and easily regurgitate the grand aims of each project, but the simplicity of the mission never translated to a simply, smoothly run project or series of projects.

On the biggest programmes I have been involved with, without fail I saw huge complexity in the multi-team, multi mini projects and distinct programmes and activities that were tied into the end delivery. Further difficulties are caused by joining a large project late; bad behaviours may have already been set and momentum and blind faith of a positive outcome entrench these bad patterns.

I have found that Silverback projects are characterised by:

- Huge budget,
- Apathy,
- Fear of not releasing a product or achieving a result that will provide a seat on a particular bandwagon,
- A thriving blame and whisper culture,
- Very long list of stakeholders and stakeholders that includes complex groups with differing and in some cases opposing motivations and desired outcomes for the project,
- Lack of a decision-making and approvals,
- Multiple work streams,
- Multiple project teams,
- Programmes within programmes.

I read a great article by Isabelle Royer (*'Why Bad Projects Are So Hard to Kill'* - Harvard Business Review) that gives an excellent insight into why large, complicated, and usually very costly projects are very hard to stop. She provided case studies such as RCA's development of the SelectaVision videodisc product - seen as 'one of the biggest consumer electronics flops of all time'.

SelectaVision research, development, production and promotion took 14 years of the company's resources and cost upwards of 500million dollars before they admitted defeat to the VHS video format and improved digital technology that came in the late eighties and onwards. It is worth emphasising FIVE HUNDRED MILLION DOLLARS! That's a huge amount of money to any business at any time in history thus far, yet this mega project rolled on and on despite evidence of a lack of return on investment and unwise use of resource.

The article author observed from the evidence that 'collective belief' in the success and value of the SelectaVision product, propelled the company for those 14 years, ultimately wasting all that money.

The article notes that once a product idea or project idea gains champions, it gains momentum, and the collective backing of a big enough group of people moves focus from gimlet-eyed analysis of value and efficiency and sweeps the project along on a wave of faith that is not necessarily backed-up by hard figures and objective reality.

My very first job in ICT was with a global engineering firm who were consulting to a German start-up that had secured the largest number of wireless local loop (WLL) 3G licences from the German government for a reported 300million

Deutschmark (DM). The start-up was called StarOne (later renamed to Star21). Star21 intended to build an Internet network across western Germany to then provide for customers Internet access services as well as cloud-based applications. Looking back on their aims, they were truly ahead of their time with their product offering. I worked with an international team of very intelligent and sharp guys from Switzerland, the US, Germany and the United Kingdom.

Hands down, it is still my favourite job, but the project was an abject disaster. Money was wasted so easily and so comprehensively it amazed me. A lean start-up it was not!

Sure, they had hundreds of millions to spend, but that won't last forever when you are building a national infrastructure, paying not one but two global consultancies (including Arthur Andersen Consulting before the Enron Scandal came to light in 2001) huge fees and day rates for a number of contractors, expanding the wireless network and Application Service Products across Germany and into new countries (Austria, Switzerland and Poland), providing breakfast, lunch and dinner each day for the large team at headquarters as well absorbing the running costs for the whole operation.

All this, while installing and testing the network in a trial and error manner. There were plenty of approved scope and installation documents that the senior managers could point to, as well as a huge repository of WLL licences and licence data and network topology specifications that would make you dizzy. I'm not kidding; I was brought into the project as one of the document control managers.

I was fresh from a professional skills course in web design and database administration and zero professional experience in IT. It was a sink or swim exercise for me and I almost sunk a few times by accidentally deleting swathes of WLL licence information from the databases I was managing. I felt like an average looking guy on a date with a supermodel – very happy to be there, but very nervous of messing it up due to lack of experience with such situations.

The scale of the intended operation was vast and the project should have been broken down into manageable projects that could be more easily controlled.

The project launched in late 1998 and eventually rumbled to a shuddering, penniless halt sometime in 2003. Even though I was a complete rookie on that project as a professional in ICT, but I looked on in wonder at the chaos around me.

In the UK and US consultants on the team, I saw a very practical – and in some cases mercenary – demeanour of just working at assigned tasks without challenging the project goals and improving progress to the end goals simply to maintain the status quo in order to keep getting paid to enjoy the perks of working on a cash-rich project in a lovely western European city (Frankfurt).

At no point did I see regular reporting on progress against the budget balance sheets and on defining the works and working to a budget and targeting product release to generate revenues to help balance the serious delivery cash haemorrhage. I never saw a project plan – for the work I was assigned or for the project as a whole. It was not clear to me at all how the disparate project teams' efforts were joined for the great cause of launching the company's products for the public.

Collective belief and a not insignificant amount of lack of project progress controls and requirements gathering ensured that the huge project was doomed to failure long before I joined the project in my small role.

Yes, I enjoyed my time on the project. Being so inexperienced in the technology sector made it a great learning experience. I thrilled to the three meals provided each day and the endless supply of fruit juice. I lived in an apartment in the city at no cost to me and explored Frankfurt every chance I could. It's still my favourite city. In hindsight as an experienced analyst and project management professional, the project was a huge mess.

Complexity of scope, allied to lack of effective intra-team-working and clear communications on progress and requirements against the project missions, and frivolous wastage of budget.

There are too many examples of poorly executed projects to shake a stick at. A topical recent example is the flurry of releases by various manufacturers rushing to jump on the iPad bandwagon (including Research in Motion's release of the Playbook, Samsung, Archos, and Dell).

Would you like to hear a great quote about the tablet market? Here goes:

"Two years after Apple's machine was launched, there is no tablet market, just an iPad market. The iPad had set a standard and the PlayBook fell short of it, and then expected customers to pay more for an inferior product. It is the kind of mistake that can doom a company."
Murad Ahmed, The Times UK (December 3 2011 12:01AM, http://www.twitter.com/MuradAhmed, murad.ahmed@thetimes.co.uk)

These manufacturers must have felt that they must quickly get involved in the brand new area so as not to be left behind by Apple. The result has been disastrous for all of them. Make no mistake that this will have resulted in tens of millions of dollars is development costs that will unlikely be recouped anytime soon.

Jeff Bezos at Amazon has a sharper approach to tablets in that he will build mid-market models and barely break even on the actual device itself - in some cases making a loss - but using the devices - (such as the much anticipated Kindle Fire) as a Trojan horse to sell more digital content to Amazon customers. This approach was considered, not a blind leap into the tablet market.

If these manufacturers had taken a similarly considered approach to releasing tablet products, I would assume that they would eventually have delivered better quality products, or chosen - on balance - not to release a tablet product. Fear of being left behind by Apple was the driving force behind the speed of the release of the tablet rivals to the iPad. Fear of missing out skews perception and alters judgment.

How to Spot a Silverback Project – extra notes

Silverback's are sometimes initiated as an emergency reaction or suggested pro-action. How else would you describe Research in Motion's (RIM) quick release and shipping of the poorly received first-generation BlackBerry Playbook tablet PC? Speed was of the essence as they sought to win market share in the market that the iPad popularised in order not to miss out on a seemingly golden opportunity in the tablet market space:

'Doomed from the start'
http://www.thetimes.co.uk/tto/business/industries/telecoms/article3246751.ece

Few Silverbacks come bigger than the failed NHS (the UK's National Health Service) IT project to create a national patient database that was awarded to the American technology company Computer Sciences Corporation (CSC) that has cost the UK tax payers billions for an end goal that will not be achieved. The Times has investigated this fiasco extensively:

'NHS computer fiasco still costing billions'
http://www.thetimes.co.uk/tto/health/news/article3251481.ece

Global computer manufacturer Dell has recently discontinued its most recent line in tablet computers. Do you feel that Dell entered the tablet market with a clear strategy and a focus on quality and consumer need? Read the interesting take by TechCrunch:

http://techcrunch.com/2011/12/05/dell-doesnt-care-about-android/

What to do? The Silverback Action Plan

"No matter how much money you throw at a project, if the people don't support it, it won't be successful. Thus, the most important metric to gauge the success of a new implementation isn't TCO or ROI, its adoption."
Michael Park, Microsoft

It is very common for project managers to join Silverback projects after the project has already started, key decisions have been made and deadlines and budgets for delivery have already been set. It is too much to ask that you will always be included at the very start of a project, so you will have to learn how to jump aboard and steady the ship that's already left the dock. If you cannot steady the ship, you must develop excellent project surveyor skills.

Silverback's usually have deep backing from a key set of stakeholders and it is this initial faith in a positive outcome of the project that sustains a Silverback project far beyond the boundaries of over-spend on budget, significant obstacles and complexities and lack of viability that would halt smaller projects or projects with more rational control structures. As Isabelle Royer found when assessing *'Why Bad Projects Are So Hard to Kill'* for Harvard Business Review, the strong believers in a project often propel the project even when logic and / or evidence dictates that they should call a halt to the project:

"...a fervent and widespread belief among managers in the inevitability of their projects' ultimate success. This sentiment typically originates, naturally enough, with a project's champion; it then spreads throughout the organization, often to the highest levels, enforcing itself each step of the way. The result is what I call collective belief, and it can lead an otherwise rational organization into some very irrational behaviour. Once a collective belief takes hold, it tends to perpetuate itself. For one thing, groups have a way of drowning out dissent."

Ms Royer proposes during this article that Project Champions should be opposed directly by an 'Exit Champion' – the voice of reason that signals project disaster and / or the need to call a halt at the current stage of the project. In the Gorilla Theory world, YOU need to act as the 'Exit Champion' when need be, as you are directly involved in the project, and your guidance should count in terms of the negative status of a project.

What to do when decisions have already been made before you are brought in on a Silverback project:

THE SILVERBACK GORILLA SCENARIO

1) Establish who ALL the project champions are and make contact. Let them know your role and that you are there to help

2) Communicate to the project stakeholders that you have identified them all and that you have identified the project champions

3) Find out EXACTLY what has been discussed, agreed and set a date with management. The person who brings you in may have some or all the answers. If not, find out via this person all the connected people and parties and get all the details you can

4) Call a halt to any work beginning or about to begin that is not of a defined scope or delivery plan. If you are working against a budget, why burn money when it hasn't been conclusively decided what the end product or result is going to be?

5) Do your own analysis of the project requirements and list all issues and unknowns. Where possible, try and create a top-level delivery plan as well as a realistic guide to compare to any dates already promised or communicated

6) Call a meeting of ALL key stakeholders (at the very least, the big decision makers/backers of the project) and map out all of your concerns. Highlight the knowledge gaps that need to be plugged so that a more accurate delivery schedule can be provided and mapped to resource plans. Highlight the likely costs against any pre-agreed budgets, and also give guidance as to best practices and how the project should be run for least pain.

In short, **GET EVERYTHING OUT IN THE OPEN** so that the

project team members are all on the same page and honest decisions can be made.

Silverback Red Alert Status Meeting To-Dos – You must leave this meeting with:

1) An agreement to accurately gather full requirements and plan properly

2) An agreement to accurately plan the delivery, based on resources, risks and contingencies

3) An agreement on establishing results/proof-of-concept gateways and early warning system.

4) If this more accurate plan has a delivery date later than the client is expecting that ways to reduce this will be discussed and if no ways to reduce the delivery sensibly can be found, then the client will be informed as soon as possible

5) An agreed process of approval and responsibility

6) If an accurate delivery plan and resource schedule is likely to show that the project will cost more than an already agreed budget, you must commit to finding this true cost as soon as possible and getting the key stakeholders to approve this over-spend

7) An agreement that where aspects of the scope from the client are unachievable within the project or unreasonable, or currently impossible, that this needs to be communicated to the client ASAP.

Do all of the above steps to the best of your ability.

If you are thrown in at the deep-end of a large, complicated project that is already happening, or about to be thrown in to the deep-end of a large, complicated project that is already happening, you need to gather status information quickly and accurately.

Here is your Silverback awareness action plan:

1) Make sure you understand EXPLICITLY what your role is and what the person(s) bringing you in want you to do. Successful and effective project managers are very flexible and proactive, bending to the needs of the project that pop-up unexpectedly, but know what your initial remit is.

2) Understand who the key players are and what the desired primary purpose and return on investment of the end product or result is

3) As quickly as possible, understand what has gone on thus far (who is/are the project champion(s), project status, any financials, planned end dates, promises made by whom and to who)
- as soon as you know as accurately as possible what is what, you need to communicate this to the project champion(s). You will be seen as the nay-sayer - the 'exit champion', but you will have to persuade these people of the credibility of what you have assessed and project

4) Ensure that there is a confirmed receipt of your assessment and prognosis by the project champion(s)

5) Ensure that there is a confirmed agreement on a way forward from the project champion(s) (even if this is an absolute - 'we are not going to change a thing')

6) If you get buy-in from the project champion(s) as to what should happen, break down the Silverback into manageable mini-projects that achieve results and give proof-of-life for the project as a whole, or help with project shutdown by revealing serious negative results that indicate that the full project should not be continued

7) Establish an early warning control system and communicate this to the team and senior management.

Make sure that there are or that you put in place control procedures (or project progress gateways) and criteria that will enable you to evaluate the project success and viability at each stage of development. These gateways ensure that progress is halted when a milestone or defined level of progress has not been achieved or is of too low quality to progress further.

Doing this enables you to catch errors and ensure that the project team does not continue to work on a stinker that will be poorly received and disappoint the key stakeholders. Make sure as best you can that the controls and gateways are clearly defined, rigorous, and – most importantly – that they are observed.

Silverback Solution Risks

The Silverback controls are far easier said than done. With Silverback projects, there will usually be a lot of money at stake, as well as pressure and a lot of prominent stakeholders with eyes on the end product. In addition, you may meet a lot of resistance as personal and/or group objectives and motivations may be competing with rational decision making as to the viability of a project or the way the project should proceed. With more people and more money comes slower decision-making, and it is very easy to miss entire mini projects within the larger umbrella project.

It is essential to seek clarification on what has been agreed or what is the desired end goal. Once you have this, you can then reverse engineer the end desire and break down as best you can what is required to get there.

To go through the steps above, you will be seen as a whistle-blower, a trouble-maker, pedantic and slow-working, incompetent and stubborn. This is usually at best. In other instances, the senior managers may seek to get rid of you as they see that you will not be a 'yes' man or woman.

There will be head-shaking and resistance to your concerns and attempt to make sense of the intended goal. The biggest risks are:

- that you will not be taken seriously

- The positive 'collective belief of the project champion(s) is hard to break

- The collective product or delivery apathy creates too many vacuums that make it incredibly difficult to bring all the project strands together to make sense of it

- The necessary decision makers do not listen and call a halt

- You are given a run-a-round and are unable to gather the necessary background information and current status information

- Different stakeholders and/or stakeholder groups have

competing motivations and do not agree on major points of the scope

Popular Silverback Examples – Hollywood Films

A Silverback Handled Well: Joss Whedon's The Avengers movie - Do I need to wax lyrical about how entertaining and well executed this film was? With a huge budget of (reportedly) over two hundred million dollars there was a lot to lose, including disappointing excited fans. The New York Times recently called the Avengers movie *"one of the most ambitious undertakings in Hollywood history"*. Kevin Feige, the president of Marvel Studios (Marvel's film division) deserves much credit for controlling all the elements that allowed a multi-franchise film to come together so well.
http://www.thetimes.co.uk/tto/arts/film/article3390866.ece

A Silverback Handled Badly: I was tempted to use the example of the science fiction (financial) flop John Carter from Mars, but I've seen the film and it is decent. Moreover, the record-breaking losses incurred as a result of the film (an operating loss of approximately $200 million) is not from reports due to shoddy filmmaking and poor production. Over-spending on the project and its marketing is one thing, but the difficult and fractured experience of making the romantic comedy Town & Country (2001) deserves mention. Co-star Warren Beatty reportedly demanded a huge number of takes for each scene, and the script was still being re-written as the movie was shooting, pushing the production behind schedule.

Two of the film's stars Garry Shandling and Diane Keaton both had to leave the shoot before the film was completed in order to do other films, and a year would elapse before the cast reunited to finish it.

Three years after filming began the movie was released to poor reviews from critics and the audiences. Ultimately the film made losses of over $100 million, making it one of the most unsuccessful movies of all time.

"When a promising project doesn't deliver, chances are the problem wasn't the idea but how it was carried out."

Isabelle Royer
(PROFESSOR OF MANAGEMENT AT "IAE LYON", UNIVERSITY OF JEAN MOULIN LYON 3)

5 THE GORILLA THEORY CHECKLISTS

"Risk is not knowing what you're doing."
Warren Buffet

Gorilla Theory is methodology agnostic. That is, the principles for avoiding trouble and aiding a smoother delivery are not linked to (and are not to be confused with) known and defined delivery and project management processes such as ITIL, SCRUM, PRINCE2, Waterfall etc.

Gorilla Theory works because it focuses on you and your project team members, helping you become more aware and proactive in terms of managing yourself when you are managing your projects, or when you are working as part of the team.

"We are what we repeatedly do; excellence, then, is not an act but a habit."
Aristotle

The checklists are designed to complement and support the insight and guidance outlined in this book. They are to be used for regular referencing and checkpoints to help improve your awareness and vigilance and allow you to find issues early, whilst helping to improve your confidence that you are on top of things. The checklists will help the good habits espoused in Gorilla Theory to stick.

The checklists are broken down into three lists:

1. **For you** (the project manager or project team member)

2. **For the project at hand** (helping to manage the project and understand the scope and the status)

3. **For start-ups/new product launches** (how will you launch your new business and deliver smoothly in the early days)

For:
Project Management
Creative Service Management
Creative and Technical Production
Resource Management
Budget tracking
Process efficiency implementation and management
Logistics
Operations

The checklists are useful to you:

If you are the Project Manager/Producer
If you are the main planner
If you are the designer
If you are the developer
If you are the client handler/account manager
If you are a key stakeholder
If you are the business owner or project sponsor
If you are the client

The checklists are available from the Gorilla Theory website at the URL below:

www.gorillatheory.com/checklists

"Genius in managing also exists. For me in football the most important thing is man management. Football for me is a human science, it is about man.

I try to prepare my players the best I can but in the end of the day they are the guys that decide everything in the right moment. They make the difference. I analyse them in a group context always but I know they are all unique."

Jose Mourinho, Multi award-winning football Coach

6 THE PEOPLE LAYER – PEOPLE SKILLS

"People like people who like them."
Kare Anderson

When it comes to influencing people to do what you would like them to do, likeability is a huge factor, and it is the factor that can determine success and failure of any project. If you provide a service or sell a product or brand, you will need to appeal to people in order to win customers and get traction. If YOU are the service, you need to get along with people and inspire goodwill and loyalty.

Traditionally, the soft skills of likeability have been marginalised and seen as unimportant compared to the more respected knowledge and methodology skills of known project management frameworks. More and more, these underrated competencies (interpersonal skills, likeability call them what you will) will determine how well you perform. More importantly, they can determine how well you are allowed to perform.

The inspiration for this book was an eye-opening project I was involved with a few years ago. In this Silverback project – the intended build of an international social platform/hub for a popular soft drink brand – a few months after I joined the project, the technology provider tasked with developing the software eventually saw the need to bring on board an experienced project manager (a SCRUM Master actually) for their operations team to help bring clarity to the workload and to better communicate development status with the digital agency I was working for.

The guy they found must have interviewed very well and impressed with his background and knowledge on delivery process and strategy. He was hired quickly after a few interviews.

He got fired after one full working day! And it was the correct decision.

Seeing the serious problems affecting the project, the guy must have decided that brutal, decisive management was required to make sense of the madness so that delivery could be brought back on track.

In short, on his first day, he was so abrasive, so rude and brusque with everybody he dealt with that on the second day, the list of complaints was so long that something had to be done. The programme director witnessed a display of the rudeness on the morning of the second day and gave the new hire a piece of his mind and fired him on the spot. A SCRUM Master was badly needed, but it had to be the right kind of person.

The guy who got fired must have believed that being pleasant was not necessary and that the project needed action. This is not practical in today's working environment of sensitive souls and oppressive workplace behaviour regulations and policy. The guy was so unlikeable that warning him would probably have not worked.

He got off to such a bad start that ill-feeling would have dogged his every interaction with the people he had so thoroughly offended. When you have problems on a project related to scope, budgets, resources, stakeholder management, unrealistic deadlines and more, adding combustible personalities who dislike each other is a problem you can do without as this will compound everything else and ensure there is not a tight-knit team focused on working together to fix the project.

I cannot emphasis enough how important people skills are. They enable you to get the best out of your team and deliver the project more efficiently. I am not stating that you must be everyone's friend, as that is not realistic in any walk of life.

Common courtesy and respect go a very long way, and if you remember to keep tabs on your moods and any issues or personality clashes with the Emotional Intelligence checklist, you will have the advantage of not allowing personal issues and behaviours – of your own or of your team members – to get in the way of delivering the project.

The Gorilla Theory People Skills Action List:

1. Write a list of project situations that bring out the worst in you and throw you off your game.

2. Write a list of personality types that bring out the worst in and throw you off your game.

3. Keep a tab on how you are feeling each day.

4. Make a note of any existing issues between project team members. Are these issues affecting the project delivery?

5. Keep a mental note to be courteous and professional with your team.

6. Keep a mental note to be empathetic with any struggles of your team members (**REMEMBER:** to empathise is good, but do not be too soft. If personal or personality issues are putting the delivery of the project at risk, then this needs to be flagged to the key stakeholders; make sure you have first discussed – or made very clear with the person(s) with the issues – your concerns. Giving them the heads-up on your concerns builds trust)

7. Listening: Learn to cultivate your listening skills as a way to get people to listen to you. Inform your project team that you are very keen on understanding their viewpoints and in listening to them. It goes a long way.

NB: Point 7 notes

Listening is a core management skill. Listening is very important whether you are the project manager or the project team member who has deliverables. I have noticed a tendency in meetings for people to compete to get their points or information across. This is somewhat natural given that most meetings have a definite time limit and people may feel that if they don't speak up (or speak over the other people or person) that they will not be heard. This is a valid fear.

What I am promoting is that where possible, you organise meetings well and plan well beforehand so that your agenda is stuck to and there is a clear structure for how the meeting should flow and then end. Give the necessary attendees a chance to speak, respond or inform, but ALWAYS keep a focus on the planned agenda points. Reign in additional or unnecessary subjects.

Erika Andersen, founding partner of Proteus International, has 3 great rules 'To Get People to Listen to You' (as published on forbes.com):

- Listen

- Get to the point quickly and simply
- Cater to your audience

Learn to lead – Grasp the Nettle

All your strength is in union. All your danger is in discord.
Henry Wadsworth Longfellow

In whatever part of a project or process that you have the responsibility for ensuring the end-delivery, try and assume the mantle of a leader.

When group action is required, leadership is a necessity. You can have all the discipline in the world and be on top of your own game, but without leadership, the other members of the team may not perform or deliver their roles as expected.

Try and set a tone and motivate. If you are the project leader, regularly communicate on progress and set a positive tone. In times of stress, when your backs are to the wall against an impending delivery date, loyal soldiers will best be able to help achieve the goals rather than unhappy and fractious team mates who care less about the end goal and even less about you and their team mates.

Some of the most successful sports team coaches are renowned motivators who instill in their players a way to conduct themselves and behave on the sporting stage. Alex Ferguson, one of the most successful managers Europe has ever produced – and coach of Manchester United football club for over twenty years – is said to be a very good man-manager, able to understand the psyche of his players and get consistently high standard performances from them.

"Leaders, more than anyone, set and spread the mood. Know your emotions; be in touch with your moods, and think of them like the common cold. If you feel infected by bad cheer, take a deep breath, recognize how you're feeling, and choose not to pass it on. Treat people with the empathy, care, and good humour that will make them feel happier, more connected, and more productive."
Peter Bregman

I used to hate interacting with team members on a regular basis. I wanted to get on with my job at my desk with as few interruptions as possible. Now I understand the importance of engaging with colleagues and understanding them and how they work and what makes them tick in some cases. I found over the years that team members are more likely to respond positively – in some cases even respond at all – to a known, friendly face or a contact known to them and a pleasant communicator.

"Emotional Intelligence is the sine qua non of leadership. Without it, a person can have the best training in the world, but he still won't make a great leader."
Daniel Goleman

You are the greatest tool in successful project delivery. Not Microsoft Project, Excel, MindMap, or a great budget and costing spreadsheet or other fancy tool. You hold the key. So, when trying to deliver a project, Gorilla Theory suggests that you roll the D.I.C.E, an acronym that breaks down the separate tasks you need to plan for and to implement to improve your task completion success rate and project management success rate:

D is for Discipline (Be consistent about being organised)
There are three i's in discipline:

I SHOULD

I CAN

I WILL

The importance and value of discipline in achieving goals could be a book of its own. Discipline is the glue that holds Gorilla Theory together.

It is very easy to be lazy or to simply not push yourself to work harder. It is no secret that hard work pays off, yet discipline continues to be a commodity that separates success from missed goals and failure. I have learnt to visualise goals as a motivator and to focus on my doing of small targets.

In the Gorilla Theory world, breaking down the word discipline means that where discipline is required, you can assess how much you have. To this end, the Three I's are very important. They help to focus on what you **should** be doing to achieve your goal or goals, what you are realistically **able** to do, and then setting a resolution on what **you will** then make effort to do consistently.

"Over time, technique wins over natural ability. People who work hard, with constant application, determination and tenacity – although they may not be as interesting, or have as much flair – will win. Overall, they will achieve a goal."
Actor, Tom Hardy

Wise words from the actor Mr Hardy. He had gained widespread acclaim in 2011 and 2012 for his roles in the films Warrior and The Dark Knight Rises. Not a naturally muscular man, he packed on over two stones of toned bulk for his roles in both films. He mentioned in interviews how the muscle building process is a tedious, disciplined routine of focus, repetition and intensity. Setting the strength and weight gain goals, doing the workouts and following the diet and supplement plan, monitoring and doing the same over and over again. Being a good project manager involves the same principles of doing the same simple things over and over again. Gorilla Theory will give the most benefit to those who can apply themselves over the duration of whichever project they are involved with or are leading.

I have learned from all types of projects that I need to be disciplined in order to avoid problems in a project. When I have either slacked-off or just not been paying enough attention, that's when accidents have happened. In the cult film classic, Glengarry Glen Ross, Anthony Baldwin's gruff, selling automaton of a character barks at the weary team of desperate real estate agents that they should 'always be closing'.

To paraphrase for project managers', you should 'ALWAYS BE FOCUSING'. Pay attention, ask questions, and make sure there is not a nasty surprise lurking in the intended delivery plan merely because you haven't asked enough questions.

If you are joining a project with defined processes, make sure you understand explicitly the delivery process and all the checks and gateways. Abide by them and use them to help you gauge what has happened, and what should happen. Checks and gateways will enable you to back-track errors and slippages too.

I have also learned to keep a daily tracker of what you need to check on or do that day. It doesn't have to be anything fancy - as simple as a scribbled note sometimes or an appointment to yourself you put in your diary, but do it. Especially when you are busy, small things and big things can be missed.

Discipline also means focusing on where you have gone wrong in the past, breaking down the detail of how you messed up and making sure you do not do the same thing repeatedly. If you make the same mistakes, you are not paying attention. If you do not pay attention to yourself, it is likely you are giving your project(s) the same loose attention. If you learn from mistakes, you certainly can get no worse and will likely become much more effective.

In the US National Basketball Association (NBA), one of its premier players - Lebron James - is being urged by experts and analysts to learn from the mistakes he made as his team (the Miami Heat) lost the 2011 NBA Finals from a winning position and as favourites in order to become the champion he craves being.

Lebron James is rated by many as the best player in the NBA, and destined for the basketball Hall of Fame, but if he never wins a championship, sporting historians will recall him as a skilful nearly man who wilted at the biggest challenges. Is it in his interest to learn what he could do better and to remedy the entrenched behaviours that reduced him in the telling games that his team lost in the finals? I would hope you all agree that the answer is a resounding 'of course!'

"**Fanatic Discipline**. Discipline can mean many things. The best-performing leaders in our study exhibited discipline as consistency of action — consistency with values, long-term goals, and performance standards; consistency of method; and consistency over time."
Morten T. Hansen

To round off the 'D' section keep in mind that discipline will help you perform better and add more value. By being consistent with the steps listed in this section you will form lasting habits that you will include in your routine naturally.

When you do good things routinely, you can focus on becoming better in more areas and becoming even more proficient. You win every way you look at it, but it does take effort. It's OK to fall off the wagon as long as you acknowledge that you have fallen and make the effort to get back on.

I is for Insight

Look under the bonnet ALWAYS. It is essential to understand the project fully. Keep it in mind that there may be a nasty surprise waiting if you don't know all you need to about whatever task or project you are working on. There is a cliché that 'only the paranoid survive'. As professor at the University of California, Berkeley **Morten T. Hansen** puts it in business terms:

"Productive paranoia is the ability to be hyper-vigilant about potentially bad events that can hit your company and then turn that fear into preparation and clearheaded action. You can't sit around being fearful; you must act."

You don't have to be a programmer to know what the code is supposed to do and how the website should be built, for example. Look past the product or mission specification to understand the background and different pieces of the product and the people who make up the delivery team and key stakeholders. This will reap dividends in most cases as it will give you access to the big picture and you will be able to see things the rest of the project team does not.

You also should make every effort to give your colleagues and project teammates a full understanding as to how you like to work and what you expect from and of them. This may sound quite pompous and difficult to do – especially if you are not very senior – but it can be done in a straightforward manner, usually with a handshake or just a quick, informal speech. It helps build a relationship and lays the groundwork for your interaction with your team. For example, I like to tell new project team members that I only approach for a verbal discussion when I really need to know something, so when they see me standing there or waiting, they should have it in mind that it is not a frivolous query or opportunity to nag that I am taking. I genuinely have something I need to know.

Just as giving an insight in to how you are and how you like to work is a very effective means of building an efficient working relationship with your colleagues, it serves you very well to understand as much as you can about how your team members operate and their personalities.

"...it is incumbent on the people who work with them to observe them, to find out how they work, and to adapt themselves to what makes their co-workers most effective."
Peter F. Drucker

Insight also means improving your self-awareness and performance. Most people usually have an incorrect view of how they are performing and what they are doing well at and what they are under-performing at. Always ask for peer and management feedback. And do this as regularly as you can. It is better to get some bracing, constructive criticism early on in a project or in your role, than get a landslide of negative comments after the project has become a disaster or you are sitting in your exit interview having been fired.

Insight also relates to honesty in communications. The desire to avoid conflict is understandable, but sometimes – particularly with projects that are going badly wrong – it is of paramount importance that searing truth be told so your project team mates and stakeholders are fully aware of issues and status. Searing truth does not mean blunt rudeness though. Lack of honesty can prolong meetings; make some meetings pointless, slow down decision-making and more.

Being forthright in a professional manner is a valuable skill and you should practice straight-talking. If you waver and sound as if you have little conviction in what you are pronouncing, then this will not help you to be heard and taken seriously. If you can lighten the blow of bad news with some levity, use it, but always emphasise explicitly:

1. What the bad status or bad news / issue or problem is, and,

2. What the consequences are of the issue

C is for Communicate

"The most important thing in communication is to hear what isn't being said."
Peter Drucker

You should always try and speak clearly, write clearly and make sure you are understood. If there is doubt in what you have said or directed, you will be blamed and things will not get done.

If you are the project manager or the person tasked with a particular deliverable, make sure that all the people who need to know the status, actions, updates, information get it and understand it. It pays to always double check and ask if you have been understood as sometimes, project team members, stakeholders or clients and customers will not understand a point and will not bother to speak up and ask for clarification or to check themselves that they understand perfectly. The onus is on you to be as granular and plain as you can so there is no confusion.

"Communication – the human connection – is the key to personal and career success. "
Paul J. Meyer

"The two words 'information' and 'communication' are often used interchangeably, but they signify quite different things. Information is giving out; communication is getting through."
Sydney J. Harris

Randy Street is a partner with ghSMART & Co, a leadership advisory firm focused on helping boards, CEOs, and executives make the right people decisions. ghSMART consultants have interviewed over fifteen thousand executives and senior managers and conducted research with the University of Chicago to determine the common traits of the most consistently successful people.

Randy gave me excellent insight into this research and his own personal observations on the executive candidates he has personally interviewed. He advises that one of the key traits of people who do very well in the workplace and are great at delivering projects is the ability to set a clear goal, and the proactivity, efficiency, and persistence to go after it.

Allied to the points above, it is tremendously important to be truthful and to demand the truth from your project team members and from the key stakeholders. If your team members believe in your honesty, you build goodwill and trust. Lying and being caught doing so quickly erodes this and positions you as being against your own colleagues and you will be able to count on less goodwill in touch project situations.

For example, if you really need to find out the status of the project to report to management or the rest of the team, and you are regarded with suspicion due to dishonesty, then you are less likely to get the truth and detailed information to enable you to fully understand the predicament. The mistrust creates a *'screw you! I don't like you, and so I don't want to help you'* attitude.

Dishonesty will count against you, as will being a bad listener. Communication is a two-way street. No matter how proficient you think you are, you will still need to listen to project team members and stakeholders to understand the scope of the project and to gather requirements. Listening is a skill – practice.

"The art of communication springs as much from knowing when to listen as it does from knowing how to use words well."
By Eugene Raudsepp *('The Art of Listening Well, 1981')*
http://www.inc.com/magazine/19811001/33.html

Project managers suffer from bad perception in many businesses. They are often seen as the annoying chasers of deadlines, who irritatingly hover over you at your desk until you give them an answer, or complete a task to their satisfaction. It doesn't have to be this way, but trust goes both ways. The person doing the task needs to own up to their responsibilities to a greater degree and be honest when asked or challenged for information or help. The project manager can display more trust and honesty as an example that can be reciprocated.

'C' can also be used for courage. Courage is regularly needed to tackle delivery issues head-on and to communicate the facts to the people who need to hear them. Courage is needed to tackle the issues that you will find with Baby Gorillas, a Troop of Gorillas, and a Silverback. Calling a halt so that you can understand precisely what the status of a project is – despite overwhelming management or stakeholder (project champion) momentum – courageous, but more importantly, the right thing to do.

I appreciate how intimidating and difficult it can be to tell senior management or key stakeholders bad news such as the delivery will be late, or more budget is needed, or the agreed scope is impossible. In my experience, the terror of imagining the confrontation is usually worse than the reality. Sure, I have had the glares, looks of daggers, swearing-under-the-breath and looks of disdain.

I learned not to take any of that personally. It does rankle at the time, and I have been very forgiving when I knew that I was partly to blame, but as you mature such things should not fester in your mind for a prolonged time. The quicker you can brush of the negativity, the quicker you can re-focus on being professional and adding value.

E is for Emotional Labour & Enthusiasm

"When you do emotional labour, you benefit: not just the

company, not just the boss, but you".
Seth Godin

I've had a job of some description since I was 19 years old. The various roles have shown me that there is a less well promoted side of professionalism that is vitally important in improving client and customer and colleague relationships.

What many a CV will have listed as 'inter-personal skills', the brilliant marketing philosopher, Seth Godin, calls 'emotional labour', the art of getting along with people.

"Like the common cold, emotions are contagious. Caroline Bartel at New York University and Richard Saavedra at the University of Michigan studied 70 work groups across a variety of industries and found that people who worked together ended up sharing moods, good and bad. Moods converge."
Peter Bregman

You can learn all the key principles of a delivery methodology but not be able to translate such knowledge into adding value and successfully delivered projects.

Experience teaches a lot, and one of the things you pick up with experience is that getting along with people is a huge help when it comes to working with a team to deliver a project. It sounds obvious, but mediocre project managers as well as proficient ones can both become far better by paying attention to emotional intelligence and improving this aspect of their management style. Ignoring other people's feelings is counter-productive whether it is in a romantic relationship, with siblings, fellow company or start-up co-founders, or your colleagues.

Seeing other people's perspective helps to approach and understand situations better. The more pressure and stress in a project, the more important it is to get positive outcomes and support from the people you are relying on to deliver the project.

In the personal checklists there is a specific one (my-ei-checklist.doc) that focuses on paying attention to both your mood and mood awareness and that of your project team members.

It is a checklist that helps you monitor how you are feeling so that you are aware that a bad mood has the potential to affect your interactions and so you can monitor your behaviour in order to keep at bay any negative or rude outbursts. In turn, the checklist helps you to pay closer attention to the emotional moods of your team mates. Paying more attention helps you to be more understanding and to alter your approach to begin to, or to continue to get the most productive output from your team.

In addition to the awareness and managing of your mood, listening is a skill that you need to hone and improve if you have previously struggled with managing a project's team members and stakeholders.

In hectic work environments, it can become a habit to speak over people in meetings or when trying to communicate a message. Another bad habit is to focus more on what you want to say rather than listening with full attention to what is being said to you. These bad habits can come to the fore in a meeting when you are focused on delivering your message or information in the time allowed for the meeting, or if you are in a meeting with dominant personalities who are hogging the floor. I have personally been in more of those types of meetings than I can remember.

I appreciate how hard it is to bide your time when you have a meeting agenda to keep and information you have to share. Let me emphasise again that listening is tremendously important.

Listening is important to connecting with your project team members. Your ability to understand the spirit as well as the information of a message, and demonstrating your understanding, is paramount in forming connections and managing effectively.

General Electric - considered one of the finest producers of business leaders in the world — has redefined what it seeks in its leaders, and it places listening among the most desirable traits in its potential leaders. GE Chairman and CEO, Jeff Immelt, has said that "humble listening" is among the top four characteristics in leaders.

Listening more is not a waste of time. Not only does it ensure that you are not missing out on key information, but will build greater connections with your team members and stakeholders. The more information you are armed with and the better the connections with your project team, the greater the chances of delivery success in alignment with the other principles of Gorilla Theory.

When the occasion calls for more authority and it is essential to get people to listen to you, I advocate the following:

1. **Be obvious and plain:** Whether in a meeting or speaking one – one, stress explicitly what information you absolutely need to communicate by the time the meeting or catch-up is over. Make it clear that if you are in a physical meeting, on the phone, via email or even instant messenger services.
2. **Be firm:** Refrain from being rude, but you need to adopt a firm tone; just as a teacher will do with pupils, or the big boss with the lower managers. Do not be embarrassed t o practice a firm speaking tone at home. If you give the impression that you lack conviction and confidence, it will be easier for other to ignore you or speak over you.

3. **Demand agreement:** Make sure you get a confirmation that what you have said or typed has been noted and/or understood. Don't let the people who need to listen disperse without any acknowledgement of the information you have given.
4. **Follow-Up:** Follow the above point by sending notes on the meeting or catch-up and what the other person(s) have agreed they have heard or read.

The D.I.C.E Action Plan

One of the quickest ways to ensure a difficult project is to be disliked – and therefore not trusted – by your project team and stakeholders. In theory, yes, it should be about only about getting the job done, but in the real world, peoples' feelings matter. A lot. Happy workers produce more than unhappy ones and are more likely to help out over and above the call of duty for a team mate they like or trust.

In terms of monitoring your own moods and performance from project to project, it is essential to your development as a project manager and happiness that you are engaged in your journey to learn more and that you will treat any negatives outcomes with a balanced mind.

I emphasise again that DISCIPLINE underpins any plan of action to ensure success or to avoid project disaster. Consistency is key and will ensure reward most of the time. Quoting Randy Street of ghSMART,

"...leaders who demonstrate these traits are called 'Cheetahs' because they identify their target and move quickly toward it. Cheetahs are successful nearly 100% of the time."

1. Use the Gorilla Theory checklists that focus on YOU and monitoring yourself.

2. Create a simple ritual that you can follow easily so that your new, improved behaviours become good habits.

3. Seek regular feedback from your team or managers to see how you are progressing with the new habits.

4. Motivate yourself. You need to tell yourself and believe that these new habits are for your benefit and they will make you better at work.

5. Document or note your progress, so you can always refer to what is working and what is not working for you.

"Success is going from failure to failure without loss of enthusiasm."
– Winston Churchill

Forming new habits will take time. The light at the end of the tunnel is an easier life in the office or wherever work is – even at home. It is not easy to stay motivated for long periods, particularly if you experience problems defining your new habits.

As Jeff Stibel advises:

"If you're not failing every now and then, you're probably not advancing. Mistakes are the predecessors to both innovation and success."
Jeff Stibel ('Why I Hire People Who Fail' - http://blogs.hbr.org/cs/2011/12/why_i_hire_people_who_fail.html)

Everybody experiences failures of some kind as they progress in life and in their careers. These hiccups help shape you and perfect good habits when you learn from what went wrong along the way.

"The best thing to happen to me in my career was to lose the finals last year. I had to change as a basketball player and as a person to get what I wanted. It was definitely. I had to learn on my own."
Lebron James, 2012 & 2013 NBA Finals MVP & Champion

7 ENTREPRENEURS AND START-UPS

"The grim reality is that most start-ups fail. Most new products are not successful.

Start-up success is not a consequence of good genes or being in the right place at the right time. Success can be engineered by following the right process, which means it can be learned, which means it can be taught."
Eric Ries, Successful entrepreneur and author of 'The Lean Start-up'.

"Any start-up needs passion and enthusiasm in order to succeed, but without a structured plan there tends to be a lot of wasted time."
(Neil Ricketts, CEO of Versarien,2012 Start-up Games Winners, Winners 2012 HP Award Manuf. Innovation,2011 Start-up Hub,MWP 2012 Best R&D)

Can Gorilla Theory help your start-up to launch successfully?

YES!

The YouTube's, Facebook's, and Instagram's of this world are making being an entrepreneur a very attractive career option for both young and older workers, and students fresh from studies. Whilst it is unwise to look up to figures such as Mark Zuckerberg, Steve Chen and Chad Hurley from a material level (the hundreds of millions of dollars burning a hole in their respective wallets), they all have one thing in common: they all worked extremely hard and focused their energies to a clear and singular mission. I'm sure that if you were to ask each of them, they would not describe project management as one of their key skills, but the success of their businesses is evidence of great effort and great focus.

Being an entrepreneur is **HARD WORK**. This needs to be emphasised. Being a successful entrepreneur is even harder work. Effective planning may be seen as boring, but it cannot be escaped, and can greatly help move you along the path to stability and profitability.

Early in my career, after gaining excellent experience on huge budget projects in the private sector during the first dot com boom, I started a business with a group of friends. It was a business services company, operating in the recruitment, payroll services and IT Support and development services. We had high hopes and the – we thought – necessary expertise. We self-funded the business initially and worked long hours to grow the business.

We were very nimble and made multiple pivots on our service offerings and internal operations. Planning was largely ignored and status checking was minimal. Speed was everything and the greatest resource we had was our motivation and stamina to get the business off the ground and to be successful.

I left the young business soon after we had generated more than a million pounds sterling in revenue (yes, we were profitable, too). The business is still around and didn't suffer the twenty four month crash that most start-up businesses do. Whilst I was there, it would have been great to have planned product and service launches better and to have a better handle on the various projects.

The problem with start-ups is that the founders and early team members and employees, tend to look at their new business more as an adventure and challenge, and less as a web of projects that need to get delivered. The latter view would bring more realism to start-ups in this economic environment whereby you have to be very sure how your money is going to be spent and what needs to get done.

Gorilla Theory is a set of principles that supports a project team; from the people who desire the end result, to the project leader / manager, and the people involved in delivering the end result of the project. In the case of a start-up, sometimes all the above groups can be one person or the people who start a new company - doing everything to deliver a new product or service.

1. Usual Start-Up Process

The Big Idea → Your Time / Your Money / Your Effort → The Product (Launch & Ops)

2. Gorilla Theory Awareness

The Big Idea → Your Time / Your Money / Your Effort → Gorilla Theory → The Product (Launch & Ops)

Start-up founders and members tend to focus on and be more excited about the business or product idea - this is very understandable. However, in the rush to be the next Last.fm, or Moshi Monsters, the next cool restaurant, hardware product, or the next Box.com, or new mass user social app, planning and awareness of the pitfalls that lie in wait in getting to product or service readiness. As a result, many start-up founders rush headlong into a new business in the hope of catching the eye of a bigger business or – in the first instance – attracting funding to help them grow.

The passion and excitement for launching a new product is a great lubricant for greasing the wheels that need to be in constant motion for a start-up, but to neglect planning and awareness will make your job harder. At best, good planning and awareness can ensure timely delivery and saving or efficient use of your starting budget – in these tough economic times, saving money is a must – no matter how much cash you have in your starting budget.

A recent convert to Gorilla Theory, Mr Lawrence Obum, spent over a decade as an investment banking professional. A CIMA-qualified accountant, he had put in hard hours on profit and loss sheets, involving complex banking products, for the likes of Credit Suisse, Citigroup, UBS, Merrill Lynch and Deutsche Bank. Over the years, he slowly grew more disengaged with his various roles and the banking culture and wanted to embrace an entrepreneurial adventure of his own.

When the UK's Companies House organisation decided to allow company registering services to happen online – directly hooking into the Companies House data for the very first time – Lawrence saw an opportunity to create an online company formation service. This, combined with his accountancy pedigree, he thought would be a winning combination.

Being an accountant, he was understandably concerned with the costs of creating a technology product. Being a number cruncher and financial controller meant that he was inclined to keep costs low and risks low. These intentions were admirable and eminently do-able when either or both of the knowledge or domain know-how are there.

The idea was to build the online service whilst still working in the banks as his 'normal job', and then taking a leap when the product was finished and generating sales. In 2009, he embarked on his journey.

Yourlimitedcompany.co.uk took well over a year to come to life from the start of the project. This was due to key factors such as:

1. The founder not having a background in technology and programming and needing a steep learning curve to get the scope of the product defined
2. The above led to a lack of clarity with Companies House's technical documentation for people wishing to use their application interfaces to build their own business registering services
3. Problematic hiring of offshore programming resources that would build the website
4. Prolonged communications problems with the chosen programmer (English was not their first language)
5. Lack of definition of how to conduct testing of the functionality
6. Limited amount of time to focus on the project due to having a demanding full-time job in the City, often working long hours in the bank.

These types of problems where there is a lack of direction in the all-important initial planning and hiring of the workers who will build the products are very common. A person without a technology background needn't be apprehensive about undertaking a technology project. If you adhere to simple rules whereby checklists control your progressing of a project by interrogating what you think you know and what you should be aware of at each stage, you can rule out or lessen some of the missteps that claim many projects or that blow(s) the intended budget of a project. Just to hammer home this last point, budget is not always measured in money.

Time is also a highly-valued currency and this relates to both yours or the business's time or a date by which you need to have your project delivered to be – for example – an early adopter to get early mover advantage in the market place.

I worked with Laurence to bring clarity to the scope of the platform that was being built and to foster a better working relationship with the offshore programmers.

I started with a simple set of checklists so that I could understand **EXACTLY** what the Companies House application interface allowed, and what Lawrence intended to build. The checklists brought a sharp focus to the current status of the project and what needed to be done in order to get yourlimitedcompany.co.uk ready and launched on the web.

This straightforward scrutiny involves unavoidable technical discussion – it was a technical project – but also plain English debate and communication of status and open question and issues and planning information.

Today, yourlimitedcompany.co.uk is generating healthy monthly sales of new business registrations for business-folk and wantrepreneurs looking to make a splash of their own just as Lawrence did. The initial pain of the project delivery has given Lawrence a great learning experience that will keep him in excellent stead for future projects, including upgrades to his website and new ones to come.

Hointer brings the power and convenience of mobile technology to the retail shopping experience. CEO Nadia Shouraboura the key to project management is speed of execution. Hointer opened their pilot store in October of 2012. It is a real store, but it is also a development laboratory.

In these early stages, software is updated and made available for customer use several times a day as the team learn more from their customers. Gorilla Theory is at play as Nadia and the management team seek project managers with a "just do it attitude, who want to have fun".

Gorilla Theory uses a specific set of checklists to help start-up founders and members to plan projects and to keep their projects on track in a way that suits the free-flowing nature of many start-ups and to be aware of risks and issues in their new business. A young business can be a blur of activity, constantly fighting fires and responding to customer or market forces feedback. In hindsight of the business I co-founded, I can clearly see the need for to take a moment to think widely of what needs to be done, what is needed, and why you are doing whatever you are doing in the first place.

Gorilla Theory is a lean project management process that is accessible to the dynamic founders and entrepreneurs and their teams who are building the new businesses of today and tomorrow.

Passion and vision cannot be learnt or bought, but if you can align this creative energy and momentum with a bit more care and planning, this can only help your start-up or business to steer clear. Gorilla Theory is deliberately designed to not be onerous so everybody can harness its principles without feeling that they need to study to benefit from it.

ENTREPRENEURS & START-UPS

Take some insight from the quotes below from a successful entrepreneur and a successful consultant who helps start-ups and established businesses.

"Investors look at two things, first the idea or the product, then the leadership team. The mix has to be right. If the idea is great, it is never going to turn into something if the founders are not real entrepreneurs. As a founder you have to have industry knowledge but also management skills. You have to have absolute believe in your product in order to convince someone else. If there is any doubt, it only means one thing: the product/idea is not ready yet. That means you have to go back to your drawing board and work on it."
Daniel Mattes, CEO and founder of Jumio, Co-Founder of JaJah

"Start-ups generally don't have a structure, or the luxury of time. The best run projects I know are completely autonomous - they require no formal project management at all, and they consistently meet or exceed targets...A start-up - in my opinion - should never attempt a large, long-term (>3 month) project. They should pare down scope mercilessly, and on a weekly basis."
Hugo Rodger-Brown, Chief Technology Officer and co-founder of Yuno Juno

Start-Up Case Study – The creation of the Bing search engine – Stefan Weitz Interview

You may find it curious that the software and technology giant is being used a start-up case study, but the creation of the Bing search engine was brought about by a new team within Microsoft, working in a very similar way to that of a start-up, researching the target market and creating a solution to challenge the competitors (such as Google, Yahoo, AOL Search et al).

Stefan Weitz is a Microsoft veteran, having been with the Redmond giant since 1997. He started out professionally as a developer and has risen through the ranks to his current position as a director of Bing Search.

He is a very early riser and professes to not needing much sleep. This is a lasting effect of his college days (not due to stress caused by being at the helm of the world's second most used search platform!).

Stefan has headed up the parts of the Bing project since its launch in 2009. The previous Microsoft Search product had a global penetration of just 7%.

Since launch, Bing has gone from strength to strength and (including the search traffic it now receives due to the Yahoo alliance) has a market share of approximately 28% - a year-on-year increase of over 400% in search volume since it launched; increased search volume equates to increased search advertising which means more revenue.

That would be a great looking graph to show the likes of chief executive Steve Ballmer and Mr G. Sure, the advertising and promotion of Bing consumes a hefty amount of the Bing budget, but the intention is growth and to build on a successful platform that is well received.

Viewed as a delivery of a high-performing and well-received new product, the project was a success. The search team business analysts found that people were very used to the search engine that they already used and were becoming increasingly less fond of search functionality 'upgrades' – greater complexity to search results. Amidst a saturated market and stubborn, habitual users, Bing was conceived and delivered and is performing much better than the previous product.

What are the secret ingredients to this well-oiled project? Stefan has been kind enough to provide the following insight:

1. What was the approach to project management within the Bing team?

FUN! A lot of fun was involved in determining how to re-develop the Microsoft Search platform. The team went back to the drawing board and did extensive research to find a direction for a new search product. The team were tasked with finding out what people wanted from search. The early findings were that a large percentage of people were jaded with search, overloaded with the seeming ever-increasing complexity of search results. The Bing team's early research indicated that people weren't looking for just a new search engine and rarely changed to a new search engine in any case.

So, the team came up with a challenge: to define a new search product designed to suit the changing needs of the consumer - a different type of search engine...but not too different.

2. Were any of the Bing project leaders effective in a Gorilla Theory way?
The Bing team was effectively a start-up unit within Microsoft, and a huge part in why the team worked so well together, feeling fully involved and engaged with the mission and having fun with a huge project was down to one man - Yusuf Mehdi.

Yusuf was the Senior Vice President of the Bing Business Group and had a remarkable ability to be transparent with his team so everyone knew the status of the project, risks, issues, and senior management feedback. He let his team know the score and did not hide from communicating with his team.

He is a guy who would have had a lot of pressure - he reported in to Steve Ballmer.

His openness had a very important, positive effect, including:

- The team members feeling included in the solution and feeling more engaged with Bing

- The team members had a greater understanding the mission goals and status

- Team members felt they could contribute to the project

- The team members had a lot of trust in Yusuf, and with their team members, putting in extra effort and trying to add more value

Microsoft - like many large companies - has had failures when it has tried to innovate and create new products (Zune, the very early tablets), but Bing is an excellent example of a large organisation innovating in a congested sector because it has to, but then taking the time to do it right and to build an effective team to get it done. As a very top-level comparative analysis, Yahoo used to be the second most used search platform, and it now uses the Bing engine for its search platform.

3. Traits you find in effective project managers
- Those who exceed training or certification they have gained (such as PMP) and go over and above to manage their projects. I like working with project managers who have three key capabilities:

    i. They are able to understand the business goals AND business requirements of a project - the entire process, including the financial impact

    ii. They are able to understand the technical scope of a project and to communicate any trade-offs that will come from a change in requirements and give the consequences of a change of plans

    iii. Project managers that understand how the finished product or service will be used by the end customer and ensuring as best they can that the product or service is robust and as usable as possible

"Good decision-making is about compressing the informational load by decoding the meaning of patterns derived from experience. This cannot be taught in a classroom; it is not something you are born with; it must be lived and learned. To put it another way, it emerges through practice."

Matthew Syed, *Bounce*

8 MAKING THE RIGHT CALLS IN A PROJECT

Being able to objectively look at the bigger picture is invaluable in project delivery decision making.

For example, web software giant, Adobe, have recently (winter 2011) stopped further development of Flash for Mobile. This is a hugely significant - and very brave - step. Sure, some people may gloat that the late Steve Jobs heavily influenced this decision by refusing to allow Flash in the Apple mobile platform, but still, it takes clear thinking to realise that to continue to go down the route of Flash Player for mobile will end in wasted time and effort and to call a halt.

What may seem to be an embarrassing climb down by Adobe, is a very good business decision that will probably save millions of dollars in development, testing and marketing efforts in a doomed effort to make Flash for Mobile as dominant as Flash for desktop websites and digital desktop applications.

I have been delivering digital projects for over twelve years. I got into project management as a means to an end, but have grown to very much enjoy what I do. I love the challenge of delivery. I have taken my fair share of knocks along the way, and for all kinds of clients and employers. I've had to be vigilant for products that have launched on Christmas day and New Year's Day, in the early hours of the morning, in foreign languages, for various government departments.

I've had to roll up my sleeves and do design work, deliver parcels, and do some programming myself to hit a deadline. I've had the shouting matches, been made the scapegoat, had furious clients at the other end of the phone line and had those stilted meetings with managers who intend to fire you at the end of the meeting.

I've paid my dues as a project manager. Swedish psychologist Anders Ericsson hypotheses that the highest levels of proficiency in complex tasks manifests itself when a person spends at least ten thousand hours practicing a particular task. This equates to roughly a decade. Some of the most interesting case studies for this rule are highlighted in the excellent book *Outliers* by Malcolm Gladwell: Mozart, Bill Gates, and The Beatles. Former England number one, two-times Commonwealth champion, and Olympian table tennis player Matthew Syed goes further with the ten thousand hour rule in his entertaining tome *Bounce* by strongly suggesting that practice is the determining factor in gaining high-level expertise. The best project managers are not necessarily born knowing how to manage Gantt charts and budgets and people. The most disorganised person can become an excellent project manager. Gorilla Theory focuses on learning and sticking with simple habits. Effective habits maketh the effective project manager.

Over the last ten years and more, I have been at the business end of hundreds of projects, managing hundreds of people and keeping an eye on millions of pound sterling worth of project budgets for clients and employers in both the private and public sectors as well as managing the delivery and setting the foundations for a start-up business as a founder and co-founder and for founders and co-founders. I've put in the magical ten thousand hours as a project manager and I am much better equipped to deliver projects. I wouldn't say that I am a master project manager as every project is different and the human element brings myriad differences to any new project. However, I can't recall the last time a project situation shocked or destroyed me. That's pretty good going in comparison to my rollercoaster early days delivering and being part of projects.

Not every budding project manager or start-up founder has the patience to wait for ten years to become a project delivery master. Gorilla Theory is intended to be a short cut (not a magic bullet) that will help you get up to speed and performing better as a delivery professional, student or worker as soon as you start reading. Having a mentor is a tremendous help in the workplace, and so let Gorilla Theory act as yours, helping you spot danger and navigate a path to improved performance and better career prospects.

I've worked with, and established tailored delivery processes in many of the recognised delivery methodologies including Agile (SCRUM, DSDM & Kanban), Prince2, Waterfall, Iterative, and ITIL in a number of businesses. I believe in the value of such structured practices as I feel that it is important to know the rules before you break or amend them. That being said, in this increasingly digital and fast moving age, the 2.0 to 3.0 businesses of the future will work to increasingly dynamic processes.

I want to help those tasked with delivering projects to become better at it and to help them be alert to processes that will help them do a better job and avoid disaster. Avoiding disaster is always good and will help your stock rise with your employer, partners, friends, clients or customers.

With particular reference to software development and building digital products (like websites, video, advertising banners and animation), delivering a product can be a very stressful task that creates tension and ill-feeling. When projects deliver late this can result in lost revenue, disenchanted employees and clients, lost business, and the premature death of a business. It could also mean that a new business does not even get off the ground in the first place.

Such negative outcomes are obviously not desirable, yet in many instances, individual project managers and businesses repeat the same mistakes project after project, month after month, year after year, never learning from these errors or understanding what is wrong with their delivery process, taking stock and then putting into place the lessons of all this delivery pain.

With Gorilla Theory, I attempt to disseminate key principles of becoming a better project manager. My hard-won experiences began first as a developer, and then as a consultant, technical analyst, technical project manager, project manager, digital producer, CTO, programme manager, and operations manager.

"If you are on the Titanic, you would be scrambling for life vests and for space on the lifeboats, not screaming at the iceberg!"

DEBRA BARONE, 'EVERYBODY LOVES RAYMOND' *TV SITCOM*

9 SUMMARY AND CLOSE

"Fear should guide you. I consider failure on a regular basis."
Bill Gates

Not every employee or business man or woman is lucky enough to have received comprehensive or structured training in project management methodologies and processes. The vast majority of workers simply work in structures and with processes that their employer dictates. Being told to do something and work a certain way is not the same as being trained and understanding the framework of how you are supposed to work. In essence, the worker untrained in 'proper' project management is flying blind in terms of how they interact with a project.

With understanding and support comes improved performance and innovation to make things even better. Gorilla Theory is borne of my long and varied experiences and is intended to help the untrained, inexperienced and experienced to improve performance within a project delivery lifecycle.

For project managers with experience and who have had difficult experiences, if you keep running up against the same problems, something needs to change. Einstein mused that to do the same thing repeatedly and expect a different outcome is the very definition of madness.

Stop hoping and praying for those factors outside of your control to come to your rescue and produce a positive outcome. Learning from past mistakes or bad experiences is very important, and self-improvement is a continual journey. The bad experiences and mistakes do not even have to be your own! If you observe performance of others and from archives and history, these can serve as teaching aids to help you safeguard your own projects moving forward. If you want to develop as a project manager outside of the traditional methodologies route, look for more areas to boost your skills.

Boosting your skills and being better at getting your tasks, projects and work done has many benefits, including winning back more of your time, making you more of a valuable commodity in the workplace, and saving money in some instances. In the workplace, more and more, you have to stand out in a crowd and add more value to an employer. As Seth Godin says:

"If you're an average worker, you're going straight to the bottom. If you're different somehow and have made yourself unique, people will find you and pay you more."

During my research for this book, I looked at great role models who have exhibited the nous and pro-activity that typifies Gorilla Theory. Ben Bernanke is one of my favourite examples because he has such a powerful and stressful role.

Ben Bernanke is described as being a nerd in a 2009 Times Magazine article ('Person of the Year 2009').

Bernanke is the chairman of the Federal Reserve, the central bank of the U.S., the most important and least understood force shaping the American — and global — economy. It is an independent government agency that controls the money supply of the United States.

Professor Bernanke of Princeton was a leading scholar of the Great Depression. He knew how the passive Fed of the 1930s helped create the calamity.

Chairman Bernanke of Washington was determined not to be the Federal Reserve chairman who presided over Depression 2.0. So, when turbulence in U.S. housing markets transformed into the worst global financial crisis in more than 75 years, he took action and injected trillions of dollars into the US economy, in stark contrast to how the Federal Reserve were passive and did not expand the money supply in the 1930s, leading the US into the Great Depression.

Did Bernanke's actions work? The US economy is still awful, but Bernanke knows the economy would be much, much worse if the Federal Reserve had not taken such extreme measures to stop the panic.

For the workers who do not realise how important they are in the dynamic of a project team, I hope that this book and Gorilla Theory has opened your eyes to ways that you can positively affect the outcomes of a delivery.

By taking the small steps of asking what is required of you and what your deliverables mean to the project, you will feel greater involvement and responsibility to your team. Strive to be a star performer in your role within a project. If you are leading the project, follow the Gorilla Theory steps of discipline, awareness, monitoring and communications to be a true leader of a project and add value. You will benefit, the project will benefit, and the business will benefit – these are all good outcomes for you.

Gorilla Theory preaches heightened vigilance, awareness, and communications skills on any project. I hope that you also take away from this book the importance of human relationships. I touched upon emotional intelligence in a previous chapter and it is an area that will be increasingly important in the workplace.

Internationally renowned psychologist Daniel Goleman – amongst many others – espouses the art and discipline of being nice: empathising with your colleagues and stakeholders, and having the social skill to manage your project team relationships to move or influence people in the desired directions is more natural for some than others. If you don't see yourself as much of a 'people person' you can work at it.

I have worked with many fellow project managers who were prized for their almost ruthless, clinical efficiency in getting projects delivered. Alloying this delivery expertise with more effective social skills will improve the value and performance of high performing delivery automatons.

"The first secret of effectiveness is to understand the people you work with and depend on so that you can make use of their strengths, their ways of working, and their values. Working relationships are as much based on the people as they are on the work."
Peter F. Drucker

If you keep on top of the management of the projects and the project people, the next frontier to focus on is the efficacy of the service or product that you are trying to launch. Another challenge for Gorilla Theory.

My countless hours of research, and the many hours of interviewing I undertook for this book has clearly shown me that a new project delivery paradigm is taking shape. Just as Google won the search war by stripping out clutter and focusing on an extremely simple user interface that produced powerful and relevant results, I believe Gorilla Theory – and its evolution – can make waves by simplifying delivery for the masses, thus winning greater engagement and efficiencies for its users. It has certainly helped me to overcome my frailties as a project manager and I have put it into practice on behalf of government organisations and multinational public companies.

I hope Gorilla Theory proves as useful to you at work, at study, and in your own time.

Visit the Gorilla Theory website to order the tailored checklists to help you in your quest for smoother project delivery (www.gorillatheory.com).

ABOUT THE AUTHOR

Henry Chuks PMP is an experienced project management professional. He has been working in the technology sector since the turn of the new millennium, his first role being in Germany at the height of the dot com boom. Graduating in Pharmacology, Henry switched careers and started initially as a web developer and database administrator, before taking on consultant and analyst roles, morphing into project and program management.

He continues to wade knee-deep into evolving technology and innovations that are shaping the business world as a whole. Having been co-founder of a successful business services start-up, he is busy working on numerous projects and advising start-ups and entrepreneurs, as well as continuing to deliver high-profile applications and websites for clients such as Barclays Banking Group and Huffington Post Media Group.

Henry is also the author of the best-selling fantasy adventure **The Lion of Umuna (The Legacy of the Nomads)** – available in ebook format and paperback.

Praise for Henry:

"Technical project manager" is a phrase that most recruiters balk at hearing, because they know how incredibly difficult it is to find anyone who truly represents that job description. We've all met people who profess to be such a thing. Maybe they once opened a HTML editor, know that AS2 and AS3 are Flash scripting languages or maybe even that it's not possible to build a fully interactive phygital project in 3 hours. Yet finding someone with both solid project management skills and a good understanding of technical issues, constraints and possibilities is difficult indeed. Unless you know Henry.

I brought Henry into Profero to work on a large-scale Change4Life project for the Department of Health (UK). It was a technical project, had a very fixed budget and we all delighted in the fact that the timelines were "aggressive". From the offset, it was clear Henry really knew his stuff. He was able to work on his own with the slightest of briefs and signposting and was able to deal with many technical queries. He managed internal technical and creative teams, freelancers, dealt directly with the Client and worked seamlessly with a third-party technical build outfit. The project was a success, on time, on budget, and much of that was down to Henry's very hard work and skill.

Importantly, Henry knows what he knows and what he doesn't know, and will ask for clarification and information when he feels his own knowledge is lacking - so you've not ever got to worry about him making technical decisions that he shouldn't be making. Unusually for a TPM, I could very happily let Henry get on with his job without worrying about any nasty technical surprises further down the line, which meant that I was free to spend my time on more strategic issues. I'm sure that last sentence will have many TDs jumping for joy, and rightly so. Henry is someone that I would very happily work with again on any kind of technical project."

- Jason Anderson, Creative Technology Director

USEFUL READING

Focus On Self-Improvement
http://www.businessinsider.com/if-youre-an-average-worker-in-this-forever-recession-youre-going-straight-to-the-bottom-2012-1?utm_source=twbutton&utm_medium=social&utm_campaign=warroom#ixzz1qLfpezWr

Tips on Managing Stress
http://msn.careerbuilder.co.uk/Article/MSN-353-Workplace-Issues-10-ways-to-manage-stress-in-a-tough-working-environment/

Improve Your Skills and don't be an Average Worker
http://www.businessinsider.com/if-youre-an-average-worker-in-this-forever-recession-youre-going-straight-to-the-bottom-2012-1

It's OK to Fail Now and Then ('Why I Hire People Who Fail')
http://blogs.hbr.org/cs/2011/12/why_i_hire_people_who_fail.html

Questions to Ask Before Approving a Project
http://www.techrepublic.com/blog/tech-manager/five-questions-to-ask-before-approving-a-project/7656?tag=nl.e053

A Silverback Project Example ('Supplier knew NHS tech project was doomed')
http://www.thesundaytimes.co.uk/sto/business/Tech_and_Media/article804316.ece

.Net Magazine: Insider Guide to Successful Website Design (Spook Studio)
www.netmagazine.com/features/insider-s-guide-successful-website-design-part-1

The Value of Emotional Intelligence in the Workplace

http://www.techjournal.org/2011/08/why-do-employers-value-emotional-intelligence-over-iq/

How to Prioritise
http://www.inc.com/lauren-perkins/how-to-prioritize-when-everything-is-a-priority.html

How to Get Focused for Better Performance
http://www.inc.com/ilya-pozin/get-your-focus-back-7-tips.html?nav=next

The Importance of Data Driven Decision Making (Increase the Chance of Success)
http://techcrunch.com/2012/04/28/data-driven-decisions-for-start-ups/

Surviving a Start-Up
A lot of stress is wasted energy when you realize mistakes and setbacks are normal. What's important isn't being perfect in business but being adaptable.
http://www.inc.com/shazi-visram/5-tips-to-surviving-a-start-up.html